FOUL DEEDS AROUND CREWE

TRUE CRIME FROM WHARNCLIFFE

Foul Deeds and Suspicious Deaths Series

Barking, Dagenham & Chadwell Heath
Barnsley
Bath
Bedford
Birmingham
More Foul Deeds Birmingham
Black Country
Blackburn and Hyndburn
Bolton
Bradford
Brighton
Bristol
Cambridge
Carlisle
Chesterfield
Cumbria
More Foul Deeds Chesterfield
Colchester
Coventry
Croydon
Derby
Durham
Ealing
Fens
Folkstone and Dover
Grimsby
Guernsey
Guildford
Halifax
Hampstead, Holborn and St Pancras

Huddersfield
Hull
Jersey
Leeds
Leicester
Lewisham and Deptford
Liverpool
London's East End
London's West End
Manchester
Mansfield
More Foul Deeds Wakefield
Newcastle
Newport
Norfolk
Northampton
Nottingham
Oxfordshire
Pontefract and Castleford
Portsmouth
Rotherham
Scunthorpe
Southend-on-Sea
Southport
Staffordshire and the Potteries
Stratford and South Warwickshire
Tees
Warwickshire
Wigan
York

OTHER TRUE CRIME BOOKS FROM WHARNCLIFFE

A–Z of London Murders
A–Z of Yorkshire Murders
Black Barnsley
Brighton Crime and Vice 1800–2000
Durham Executions
Essex Murders
Executions & Hangings in Newcastle
  and Morpeth
Norfolk Mayhem and Murder

Norwich Murders
Strangeways Hanged
Unsolved Murders in Victorian &
  Edwardian London
Unsolved Norfolk Murders
Unsolved Yorkshire Murders
Warwickshire's Murderous Women
Yorkshire Hangmen
Yorkshire's Murderous Women

*Please contact us via any of the methods below for more information
or a catalogue*
WHARNCLIFFE BOOKS
47 Church Street, Barnsley, South Yorkshire, S70 2AS
Tel: 01226 734555 • 734222 • Fax: 01226 734438
email: enquiries@pen-and-sword.co.uk
website: www.wharncliffebooks.co.uk

Foul Deeds Around
CREWE

Peter Ollerhead and Susan Chambers

Wharncliffe Books

First Published in Great Britain in 2010 by
Wharncliffe Books
an imprint of
Pen and Sword Books Limited,
47 Church Street, Barnsley,
South Yorkshire S70 2AS

Copyright © Peter Ollerhead and Susan Chambers, 2010

ISBN 978 1 84563 107 9

The right of Peter Ollerhead and Susan Chambers to be identified
as authors of this Work has been asserted by him in
accordance with the Copyright, Designs and Patents Act, 1988.

A CIP catalogue record of this book is available from the
British Library.

Printed in the United Kingdom by
CPI Antony Rowe, Chippenham, Wiltshire

Pen & Sword Books Ltd incorporates the imprints of
Pen & Sword Aviation, Pen & Sword Maritime, Pen & Sword Military,
Wharncliffe Local History, Pen & Sword Select, Pen & Sword Military Classics,
Leo Cooper, Remember When, Seaforth Publishing and Frontline Publishing.

For a complete list of Pen & Sword titles please contact:
PEN & SWORD BOOKS LIMITED
47 Church Street, Barnsley, South Yorkshire, S70 2AS, England.
E-mail: enquiries@pen-and-sword.co.uk
Website: www.pen-and-sword.co.uk

Contents

For all the members of Crewe's Historical and
Family History Societies

Chapter 1

Early Tales of Murder and Mayhem

The modern town of Crewe, born with the coming of the railways in the first year of Victoria's reign, is a recent development compared to the neighbouring ancient market towns of Middlewich, Nantwich and Sandbach. In a way of life that changed very little for centuries, the people of south-east Cheshire would bring their cheese, pigs, chickens and linen to the bustling markets in these old towns. A few scattered farms and cottages occupied what we now think of as Crewe town. It was in earlier times known as Monks Coppenhall, a township adjacent to the old Crewe manor in the neighbourhood of Crewe Hall. Villages and hamlets were dotted around this part of the flat Cheshire plain where people lived in thatched timber-framed cottages, tending a few animals and growing crops to keep their families. Oak woodlands flourished on the clay of the surrounding countryside, and provided timber as fuel for the salt workings of Nantwich and Middlewich, while good crops of grass meant plenty of milk for Cheshire cheese production.

Crime has always been an inescapable part of life and even in these peaceful Cheshire hamlets there were early glimpses of acts of violence. There is little trace now of the mill pond and mill cottage that once stood near the Valley Brook as it weaved its way through Barthomley, though the area is still rural. A violent killing took place there in 1260 when Richard the miller was brutally stabbed with a sharp weapon and died in his wife's arms. The culprit was a local man, Osbert, who then went on to steal the couple's mare. Osbert claimed that he had killed Richard because he had stolen clothes from his house, but the court at Chester sentenced him to hang. In the same year an Acton woman by the name of Ammera was accused of burglary and hanged, as was Nantwich man William Chapelein, a horse thief. After his trial at Chester Chapelein was handed back to the bailiffs from Nantwich, who took up the offer of the loan of the use of the gibbet 'as the day was nearly over'.

In these early days the tranquil rural Cheshire scene was from time to time shattered by gangs whose lawlessness was notorious throughout England. In the late 1300s Cheshire men were frequently making armed raids into Staffordshire and Shropshire, robbing, raping and murdering, then heading back home with the booty. They felt safe in the knowledge that they could not be tried outside the county and that there was a good chance they would be pardoned by the King for crimes committed within Cheshire, which was one of the few counties at that time that was more or less independent of the rest of the country, being a 'county palatine'. A commission during Richard II's time reported 'malefactors who wandered about the county to the terror of the inhabitants'. Disputes between local factions were common, kinship ties were strong and often gangs comprising followers of leading families, their tenants and friends were involved in fierce battles over land. In fact, the gentry were frequently the perpetrators of many of the crimes committed and there were no nobles resident in Cheshire to maintain some kind of control.

The Sheriff was the county's chief legal official and staff included sarjeants, who had the liberty to behead robbers on the spot if caught in the act. A County Court met eight or nine times a year, and there was also a travelling court held by the Justice of Chester, known as an 'eyre'. These were held annually over one week in the various hundreds with a local jury; the Nantwich session was always the last to be held, on Saturday and Sunday. (Cheshire was divided into seven 'hundreds', in use for various administrative functions until the nineteenth century.) The majority of cases were offences 'against the peace', and assaults in 1354 were reported as being committed with sticks, knives, axes, a rake and a fist. William de Crewe was fined because he didn't turn up for the court, contrary to his tenancy agreement.

In 1407 a prominent Coppenhall family was involved when a gang led by Nicholas Parker murdered Justice of the Peace Thomas Malbon from Bradeley Hall, just over the township boundary in Haslington. Few details of the case survive but it is recorded that Parker was outlawed, which meant he lost any protection from the law and had his lands and goods seized by the Crown. This was often the punishment meted out to those who could not be found and brought to court, and was no doubt preferable to the gallows. This was the fate of many who committed not only murder but any 'felony' which included rape, arson and robbery. Cattle stealing was a common offence that could be punishable by hanging, and Lawrence Priestwood, who stole five bullocks in Woolstanwood in 1463, suffered that punishment at Chester. Some Coppenhall men (including another Parker) who were also accused of stealing cattle a few years earlier had managed to persuade the jury that they were not guilty.

From 1536 Cheshire was obliged to have Crown-appointed Justices of the Peace in Quarter Sessions; in addition to their judicial duties, their powers included preliminary hearings of more serious cases for the assizes and the administration of local government. Cheshire miscreants were tried in Quarter Session Courts held in different towns around the county – Chester, Northwich, Middlewich, Knutsford and Nantwich.

Day-to-day guardianship of local affairs was in the hands of township constables, the most important of the township officials who were chosen at the local Manor Courts and every man was supposed to take his turn at this. The constable was expected to maintain the stocks, pillory and whipping post for

Haslington Hall, home of the Vernon family, lords of the manor.
(Cheshire Archives and Local Studies)

punishments and the local butts for archery practice in case of invasion and generally do his best to maintain law and order. Every town and village had to have its pillory or stocks for punishing relatively minor incidents and had to report to the Quarter Sessions every year that these were in good repair. In 1603 it was decreed that 'In every township a whipping stocke is to be set up before the next meeting of her majesty's justices'. It was also stipulated that vagrants were to be stripped naked from the waist up for whipping (rather than totally naked as previously).

For many centuries one of the principles of punishment was that the inhabitants of a town or village should witness it and learn lessons from it. In the late 1500s in Nantwich there was a cage in which a man suspected of fornication was punished. A cucking stool was a device designed to give a good dousing to a noisy, troublesome woman by plunging her into a river or pond, and it was believed this would cure abuse and nagging. These are recorded as being in use in Sandbach, Nantwich and Cholmondely.

Fear of 'rogues and vagabonds' was immense, an ever increasing horde of wanderers who no longer had the charity and alms of the monasteries to depend on after Henry VIII closed them down. Innkeepers were warned not to give lodgings to these people and would be taken to court if they did. Many poorer people no longer had the freedom to pasture their animals and grow the family's food on common areas, as these were rapidly being enclosed by landowners and shared out amongst those who already owned land. A series of bad harvests in the 1590s was another factor that made life difficult for poorer folk. The 1597 Vagrancy Act stipulated that dangerous rogues could be dispatched overseas, and this facility developed into the frequently used system of transportation over the next couple of centuries.

A vast array of miscreants and their crimes were presented to the magistrates every quarter, some that were within their power to deal with, others were passed on to the assizes, the higher courts held at Chester. In the 1590s, the people of Wybunbury must have been pleased when a notorious keeper of a tippling house, Michael Mullington, was finally brought to court. A man of evil repute who harboured and supported sundry 'evil and lewd persons', he illegally sold ale and food unchallenged even while divine services were being held, due to the fact that he threatened his neighbours with violence if they dared consider complaining. He had brought up in his family a youth by the name of Richard Barlow, another local criminal whose daily occupation, together with Mullington's son, was to track down rabbits and hares and illegally kill them with staves. They also poached partridges and fish from local fishponds and stole horses, pigs, geese, hens, hay and fuel for fires from neighbours' houses after dark.

Another infamous local was Thomas Winterley, a Haslington barber and well-known drunk. He assaulted Lawrence Taylor several times and on one occasion came to his house while he was out and tried to rape his wife, who eventually managed to bar the door against him only to have him attack it with an axe. He had, in fact, at one time been imprisoned for stabbing some of his neighbours and consequently was said to harbour a grudge against the community.

John Smith, again of Haslington, was one of a gang of half a dozen men who used swords, daggers and canons to create mayhem there in the 1590s, putting people in fear of their lives. The same armed gang broke into William Leversage's wood, Roughcroft, in Haslington, wreaking havoc and stealing timber and valuable sparrowhawk chicks.

In fact, Haslington seemed to suffer more than its fair share of criminal activity. Since the 1560s Sir Thomas Vernon, who lived in Haslington Hall, had been the lord of the manor and he too kept valuable hawks in Oakhanger Wood. Hawking was a popular pastime amongst the gentry and the birds were very valuable, and for several years Sir Thomas had experienced problems with people stealing from the nest, so a constant watch was kept on it by a rota of servants. One evening at dusk in May 1603 suspicious activity was noticed by one of the servants, Thomas Wilkinson. He saw local man John Booth go into the wood and head straight to the tree with the nest and climb up it. Nabbed by Wilkinson, Booth made the excuse that one of his mother-in-law's goslings had been killed and he was going to destroy a kite's nest (this bird of prey was regarded as a nuisance at the time). Wilkinson manhandled him out of the wood and found he had a bowl for the chicks hidden under his doublet, whereupon Booth fell to his knees and pleaded with him not to tell Sir Thomas. He offered a noble (33p) to him to forget it, and then upped it to an angel (50p). These bribes were refused and en route to Haslington Hall they stopped at Booth's mother-in-law's cottage and she joined in the pleading and offered further bribes. Wilkinson proceeded to take them towards the Hall, climbed over a stile leaving Booth and the old lady on the other side, whereupon Booth took flight back into the woods with his mother-in-law preventing his pursuit by the diligent servant.

In 1602, towards the end of Elizabeth's long reign, there was trouble in Warmingham, Sandbach and Middlewich from a gang led by Robert Sponne. He was a notorious thief, robbing his neighbours of valuable timber and corn from their barns and fields and letting his cattle graze on other people's grass during the night. He had been lucky to avoid the hanging that some of his confederates had recently suffered for burglary. To divert attention from his activities, he maliciously accused innocent neighbours and also claimed that there were threescore other men in the Cheshire who were as evil as his hanged mates. The locals were terrified that Sponne might commit some outrage such as burning down their houses or killing their precious cattle.

Warmingham was not always as tranquil as it appears in this view. (Cheshire Archives and Local Studies)

The busy market town of Nantwich provided ample opportunities for troublemakers. In the early 1600s John Wood and William Clowes, well-known drunkards and haunters of ale houses, caused a great tumult in the market place on several occasions. In one incident they almost killed people by pulling down a market stall in front of a shop where a chapman (trader) had his wares on sale, resulting in these being flung into the street. The shop itself belonged to William Lea who every market day had to suffer his customers being frightened off by the brawling of these men, and their threats to pull the whole building down. The final straw came one Saturday when they commandeered some horses laden with sacks of corn on their way to the corn market and led them inside Lea's shop and shed the loads.

Witchcraft, or at least accusations of it, occurred in Nantwich on a couple of occasions in the seventeenth century. In 1650 widow Katherine Davies was said to have bewitched to death a black calf worth 7s and several children, including 8-year-old Richard Bromhall who died within five days.

Another case involved Mary Briscoe, wife of Thomas Briscoe, a Nantwich horse-collar maker, who was tried at Chester in 1664 for exercising devilish arts. She had been involved in a long dispute with a neighbour, Ann Wright, over the tenancy of a house in Nantwich, and seems to have been a somewhat aggressive personality. She had threatened Ann after she would not give up the house to her, whereupon Ann's son fell ill and died within three months. The quarrelling over the house continued and one day Ann's 12-year-old daughter was playing outside and suddenly rushed home having been very frightened by the strange appearance of Mary Briscoe's eyes, which she claimed seemed to be as big as saucers and of many different colours. She fell down in a fit, and reportedly languished for six months and then died, often complaining in her illness that Mary Briscoe was tormenting her and pricking her with pins and needles and nails. It was claimed by a couple of witnesses that the child's eyes sometimes came out and rolled on her face. Even Mary's husband was troubled by the possibility that his wife was involved in witchcraft, saying that she was acting just as her mother had done – and she had been hanged for witchcraft some years before.

Strangely enough, it was Ann Wright who first appeared in court, namely the Consistory or Church Court in Chester, charged with unjustly calling Mary a witch. It emerged that the two neighbours had been engaged in a series of squabbles and rows over the last four or five years, and that Ann had already been charged with slander against Mary for saying she had someone else's husband in her house while her husband was away. Sir Thomas Mainwaring, one of the Nantwich magistrates, had already tried to broker peace between the two women. A succession of witnesses told various tales of babies out of wedlock, lost husbands and allegations that other witnesses had been bribed. It was revealed that Ann's daughter who had supposedly been bewitched had in fact for several years been suffering from 'the King's Evil', a form of tuberculosis of the glands of the neck. The witchcraft charges were not taken seriously, and Ann was ordered to stand in front of the minister's reading desk in Nantwich church and apologise for doing Mary Briscoe much wrong.

However, a couple of months later Mary appeared in the Chester Assize Court charged with bewitching three people, including Ann Wright's daughter, though she was eventually found not guilty and died twelve years later after taking poison.

The Church Court, held in Chester Cathedral, had a specialised role in the legal system, dealing with misdeeds of a 'moral' nature, though this covered quite a range of actions including complaints about the behaviour of the clergy, sexual matters such as fornication, adultery and incontinence, rows about church tithe payments and the important category of 'defamation'. A good name and reputation were very influential in the seventeenth and eighteenth centuries and numerous cases were brought before the Church Court, including one concerning rowing neighbours in Middlewich in the 1730s. Ann Whishaw took neighbour John Earle to the court for calling her an 'impudent whore' in the street one day. Claim and counter claim followed and various neighbours gave their version of events, including the next-door neighbour (presumably a red-head) who claimed to have recently been called a 'carrot-pated whore' by the same man. Ann's mother, who lived in the same house, complained that Earle's children were always relieving themselves in front of her house. A salt officer who was a lodger in Ann's house was quoted as saying that he in fact frequently had sex with her, and that her mother often left *her* bedroom door open for him too. Ann did have a bad reputation in Middlewich and beyond and he claimed that her own stepfather called her a whore.

Another case of defamation had been brought a few years earlier by Thomas Ellison. He had been working in Weston with one of his men when Randle Wheelock came up and they got into a row over a watercourse. This resulted in Wheelock making accusations that Cromwell was the godfather of the two men, and that they were two of the falsest traitors to the King in England. People were very sensitive about this sort of allegation after the restoration of the monarchy in the form of Charles II. In Cromwell's time it had been seen as defamation to include the phrase 'Cavalier rogue' for an insult, and a Coppenhall man had been presented to the Church Court for using that phrase.

Another problem that resulted in many cases was seating in churches. Each property was allocated a pew when seating in churches became the norm, and this led to frequent arguments and often violence, sparked by religious and hierarchy disputes. In 1638 at a funeral in Wrenbury George Taylor, wearing riding boots with spurs, went into William Cudworth's pew and sat on him and pushed him roughly into a corner injuring his legs and causing him to suffer for several months. There were several incidents in Coppenhall church (the old timber-framed building that stood on the site of the present St Michael's), including one in 1639 when during a service Robert Shenton suddenly leapt over several seats and violently pulled a local tailor out of his seat. A few years earlier seating problems between two Coppenhall gentry families, the Malbons and the Fullshursts (from Shaw Hall), were settled after a hearing by the Church Court by the simple expedient of allowing two Fullshursts servants to sit in one end of the 7ft-long pew and the Malbons in what space remained. Both these prominent local families feature in other incidents over the centuries which are recorded in this book.

Chapter 2

Medieval Monks and Feuding Families

A medieval monastery traditionally represented an oasis of peace and calm, a centre of scholarship and prayer, a place for healing the sick, giving succour to the poor and rest to pilgrims. Combermere Abbey was no doubt recognised as such a haven in its early days but over the years the air of peaceful sanctity dispersed and the abbey gained a reputation for crime, litigation and quarrels which pursued it throughout much of its four-century history.

The abbey was founded in 1133 by Hugh Malbank, son of William the first baron of Wich Malbank (Nantwich), who had come from Normandy soon after William the Conqueror. Hugh was a powerful man, with much land and influence, including a castle in Wich Malbank, and like many such men he hoped for spiritual benefit and a guarantee of prayers for the souls of him and his family by establishing a religious foundation. It was originally given to the Savigniac religious order but later taken over by the Cistercians. Hugh Malbank gave them a wooded site with a mere in Wilkesley on the southern border of Cheshire, together with several nearby manors, woods, mills, fisheries and churches, including Acton church and what was then its chapel in Nantwich. He also granted the right to pasture animals throughout Cheshire, the right to take wood for building and fires, a quarter of the lands of the town of Nantwich, income from the salt (a precious commodity) and a supply of it for the abbey. Many other wealthy landowners in the area also eventually gave lands and various benefits, including John de Mere of Coppenhall.

These generous donations should have ensured a comfortable income of rents and taxes for the abbey, but within less than a century problems arose in the form of disputes over the original gifts of land, especially by the heirs of those that had made the original donations and were now quibbling over their ancestors' generosity. There have even been questions asked in very recent years as to the validity of the original foundation charter, supposedly issued by Hugh Malbank – the monks may have found it necessary to forge a charter to protect their interests in the face of challenges from various authorities including the King's justices. There were also frequent quarrels with nearby religious houses such as Dieulacres near Leek, where there were arguments over the rights to pasture the abbey's animals, and Buildwas Abbey near Ironbridge concerning who had the rights to use various granges where the crops were stored.

Combermere Abbey, built as a home for the Cotton family after the destruction of the monastery. (Cheshire Archives and Local Studies)

Income was raised from general agriculture, sheep farming and wool production but by 1275 there were serious debt problems and a few years later the abbey's short-lived possession of 'Monks' Coppenhall was exchanged for £213 by Bishop Robert Burnell, an influential advisor of Edward I, who then became its lord of the manor. The abbey would have been taking revenue from land it leased out to other people in Coppenhall and fees paid by the locals for having their corn milled at the water mill. It is doubtful that Burnell took much personal interest in the welfare of Coppenhall as he owned the lordship of dozens of manors. The Crown had to take over the affairs of the abbey on more than one occasion, such as in 1315 'on account of its poverty and miserable state' and repair work was ordered.

The dozen or so monks were sometimes involved in local disturbances, which is unsurprising given that these were often lawless times. An incident occurred in Nantwich in 1309 when a gang led by Richard Fullshurst, lord of the manor of Edlaston near Nantwich, attacked the abbot and murdered the prior, burned down some houses that the abbey owned and stole money from the abbey. An enquiry was ordered but before it could be heard Fullshurst launched a violent attack on the abbot and his servants in his house, killing three horses and again stealing money. The abbot was too terrified to return to the abbey for a good while. Fullshurst subsequently made complaints about the abbot to his superiors and Edward II found it necessary to intervene. Further stories of violence followed throughout the fourteenth century, and in 1360 the abbot of the time was accused of organising an attack on the property of Richard's son Robert Fullshurst. Robert was lord of the manor of Crewe and Barthomley, having married Elizabeth Praers, the heiress of the manors. There was further trouble twenty years later when one of the monks, apparently something of a criminal character as he was later outlawed, was accused of stealing from the abbot.

Debt problems still haunted the abbey in the 1400s, and by 1410 it was reckoned that if the abbey actually paid all its debts it would have no money to live on, thanks to the poor management of earlier abbots. In 1414 the abbot was accused of forging gold coins, presumably an act of desperation. Just three years later two Shropshire men were charged with carrying out a violent attack on the abbey and making off with bibles and valuable books. In 1446 a labourer from the nearby hamlet of Dodcott killed a subsequent abbot by a shot from an arrow, probably as part of a local riot.

It is perhaps only fair to point out that Combermere was not the only abbey with problems. St Werburgh's in Chester had some abbots who were far from law-abiding. The monk who became abbot in 1455 was frequently in trouble for not keeping the peace, and had been charged with various offences. He was at one time imprisoned in Chester Castle and was along with some of his monks often involved in disputes with the city authorities.

The disputes and financial problems of Combermere continued and in 1520 in a desperate attempt not to further damage the monks' reputation a murder on the premises was kept secret for several months. John Jenyns, a tanner who worked in the abbey, stabbed a monk by the name of Dan Ottewell with his dagger and killed him. The body was taken by several of the other servants to a bedchamber, and they then set off to apprehend the murderer; however, the prior stopped them, saying 'This abbey is already in an evil name for using of misrule', and made them all swear that they would not reveal the murder. Jenyns carried on working in the abbey as a barker, stripping bark off timber for use in processing leather, for six months until word got out and he was arrested and taken to the gaol in Chester Castle by Thomas Sounde. The last we hear of the case is that no one could be found locally who was actually willing to indict Jenyns so the case was dealt with in the Court of Star Chamber in London.

In 1536 agents were dispatched by Henry VIII to report on conditions in religious houses. Their accounts were often exaggerated in an attempt to justify closure of the monasteries by Henry and claims that four Combermere monks were guilty of 'sodomy' was perhaps an example of this, though in fact it did not compare too badly with the reports of sexual habits from many other such foundations. The abbey was closed in 1539 in Henry's dissolution, and much of it destroyed before the land was given to the Cotton family who built a house there, part of which incorporates the remains of the abbey.

The powerful Fullshurst family, who, as mentioned earlier, had had their problems with the monks of Combermere, were involved in further violent disputes nearly two centuries later. The family were lords of the manor of the old Crewe township from the 1350s to the 1570s, living in the earlier Crewe Hall, which by the sixteenth century was in very poor condition. As was often the custom in these times, the family took the law into their own hands when the ownership of three fields on the borders of Wistaston and Monks Coppenhall, just outside their own manor, was in dispute in 1530. The tenure of the land had been fought over fourteen years previously when a court decreed that William Bryndley was the rightful occupier rather than the Fullshursts. A challenge was made to this legal decision when an attack was mounted on the orders of Sir Thomas Fullshurst, lord of Crewe and past sheriff of the county, by a gang of sixteen of his men in an effort to reclaim the fields and woodland for his family. The gang cut down thirty-six trees growing on the site, and made huts and cottages for themselves on the land with the timber, guarding against it being retaken.

Bryndley also had pasture land in Monks Coppenhall in the area of the water mill and the mill pool where Stewart Street now stands, next to his Wistaston lands. A gang of eight armed men from Monks Coppenhall, including another of the Fullshursts, Francis of Shaw Hall in Coppenhall, ejected

Bryndley from his land and beat up his daughter and a servant who were working there. The same Francis, seven months later, stole five of Bryndley's cattle from the pasture land, one of which he immediately slaughtered and butchered for the use of the Fullshursts at Shaw Hall.

Family loyalty and 'kinship' were prominent features of life in medieval and Tudor times and were demonstrated in the town of Nantwich on a couple of occasions. In 1542 Edmund Gryffin of the mansion house in Batherton, a small manor near Nantwich, was assaulted by a gang of about fourteen men, notable amongst them being shoemaker Thomas Crewe and John Walthall, capper. The others included five other shoemakers, a glover and a couple of local 'gentlemen'. In fear of his life, Gryffin took refuge in John Spele's house, where he was pursued by the gang, only to be saved by Thomas Maisterson, magistrate and steward of the town, who intervened and put a stop to the violence.

Gryffin made an official complaint about the attack to another magistrate, Richard Hassall, only to discover that Hassall, being a kinsman of Thomas Crewe, did nothing about it. When the case was finally examined Crewe and Walthall made the well-known response, that Gryffin had started it and they were defending themselves.

Family loyalty is well illustrated by a notorious case from Nantwich in 1572, featuring some of the same families. There had been many disputes over land (always a precious commodity) between Nantwich families for decades, and they often resorted to violence as a quicker way of resolving disputes than going to law; family, friends and servants were always on hand to assist with easily acquired weaponry.

A notable building in present-day Nantwich is the Crown Hotel, a timber-framed inn dating from the time of rebuilding soon after the disastrous 1583 fire, which destroyed much of the town in that area. The landlord of the Crown in the early 1570s,

Roger Crockett, had caused a huge controversy and some excitement by securing the lease of a field before the current lease, held by Richard Hassall, had finished or been renewed. The land in question was Ridley Field, pasture land where Queens Drive now stands, the owner being Edward Leigh of Leicestershire. Amongst many local people supporting Hassall in the feud were John Maisterson and Richard Wilbraham, of notable Nantwich families related to his by marriage. They were all, in fact, wealthy families who had accrued money from salt making, the Maistersons having been in the town the longest.

There had been ill-feeling and bitterness over the tenancy of the field for a few years, involving the fathers of the two main protagonists, and Roger Crockett had got to the stage where he was reluctant to cross the bridge over the river into Welsh Row because of the hostility. Thomas Wettenhall of White Hall, a later version of which stands in its place in Welsh Row, complained that when he was sitting in his garden with Crockett, they had to

The Crown Hotel, Nantwich, as rebuilt after the great fire in 1583. The landlord of the original inn was attacked and killed in 1572. (Susan Chambers)

put up with abuse shouted by Hassall's wife, yelling from the doorway of her house where she was sitting. She had called Wettenhall's wife 'a boare' and labelled his new house 'the Tower of Babylon'. Townspeople had worked themselves up to quite a pitch over the matter, many of them being related by blood or marriage to Crockett or Hassall, or working for or even being a tenant of one of them and therefore owing allegiance. Crockett had received numerous threats including one that his bones would be broken if he went near Hassall's house along Welsh Row. Some people were of the opinion that Crockett himself was 'an honest quiet fellow' and that the troublemakers were the Wettenhall bothers and in particular Brigit, Crockett's wife. One of the servants from the Crown had heard gossip from one of the maids coming back from milking that there would be lot of mischief if he took over Ridley Field, and reported this to Crockett.

Crockett was due to take over the tenancy of the field on 19 December, and Leigh's men had arrived in the town to clear Hassall's cattle from Ridley Field. At around 8 o'clock in the morning Thomas Wettenhall was walking along Wood Street towards his own pasture to do some work when he was attacked by Thomas Wilson, one of Hassall's tenants. Wettenhall's brother Roger, hearing of the assault, came hurrying towards the spot and was himself attacked by Edmund Crewe and Hassall. A general brawl then followed, someone was armed with a fire shovel, some of them with pykes, and as a result Roger Wettenhall was quite badly injured, ending up lying on a hedge.

Crockett then came rushing into the street with a staff and was immediately set upon by Edmund Crewe with a blow to the head, which knocked him to the ground and caused him to bang his head. A couple of women went to his aid and tried to get him to stand, when on the scene appeared Richard Wilbraham, a respected gentleman of the town and a cousin of Hassall. He was half-dressed, and without shoes, having heard the noise from his house around the corner in Welsh Row, but he took command of the situation and calmed things down. Crockett was obviously badly injured, presumably with a fractured skull. There were numerous marks on his body; an eye had been damaged, blood was coming from his ear, nose and mouth and he was reported to have vomited 'his braynes and blood'. He was helped back across the bridge to the Crown, but by that evening he was dead.

It soon became obvious that Hassall had been planning violence against Crockett and friends. About twenty people gathered at Hassall's house after the attack, where there were said to be numerous bylles and staves stacked in the hall and parlour and one of his maidservants had been seen taking a dagger covered by her apron to the cutler to be sharpened.

Soon after Crockett died, Thomas Wettenhall asked a local painter, John Hunter, to do a picture of his body with all the marks on it. The plan of the pro-Crockett faction was to assert that he had died as a result of numerous blows rather than the 'tapp' he had received from Edmund Crewe, and several men began to be named including Richard Wilbraham, who had in fact broken up the fight. Crockett's wife had his naked body displayed in the street for everyone to see the multitude of injuries and bruises all over his body, including a huge wound on his chest.

Meanwhile, Edmund Crewe (one of many Crewes in Nantwich at the time) disappeared from the scene, first sent to the home of Hassall's brother-in-law in Wrenbury, then on to Northwich, then Sneyton Wood and out of the county, aided by various friends with money. There was some reluctance on the part of the local law enforcers to take action, but eventually a group of Hassall supporters, including Wilbraham, were arrested.

On the following Saturday the body, by now smelling most unpleasantly, was brought into the market place, the bustling centre of the town, perhaps even busier than usual as it was nearly Christmas. It was then taken into the church for the coroner's inquest, the chief coroner being John Maisterson, a Hassall supporter. Another coroner was John Minshull, of the same faction. The picture of the putrefying body had to be amended by John Hunter to add the blood that suddenly issued from its nose, mouth and ears after it was moved into the church.

A vast amount of evidence was taken and a manslaughter verdict was recorded by the coroners, partly because there was an understanding that Crockett had brought things on himself by his unfair dealings over Ridley Field. The Hassall faction insisted that death had been caused by the single blow of Edmund Crewe who had disappeared so could not be charged.

Brigit Crockett was determined to lay the blame on Richard Wilbraham, who had in fact broken up the fight, despite being a kinsman of Hassall. She appealed to the court in Chester. Her servant Thomas Palin was bribed with the offer of a choice between three houses when he got married, on condition that he would testify that he had seen Richard Wilbraham strike the fatal blow. He went to Chester to do this and was arrested, sentenced for his sins and only saved from the gallows when he recanted. The widow Brigit was so determined to pursue justice that the corpse was dug up after a few weeks for the wounds to be re-examined. Finally, she attempted to bring a murder charge against the whole group including Hassall and Wilbraham in the Court of Star Chamber in London, but without success.

Chapter 3

Transportation for Troublemakers

*We complain against Thomas Knutsford for annoying us in a
filthy and beastly manner with the excrements of his house of
office [privy], sweeping it to run through my hovel [shed] and
towards Howells house & so into the street to the church wall
contrary to reason and neighboushippe.*

So stated Robert Wickstead of Nantwich at Lord
Cholmondely's Manor Court in the 1660s. The court
obliged Thomas Knutsford to do something about this
sewage problem by a certain date or face a fine in the Manor
Court. More serious crimes were the business of the magistrates
or assize judges; the Manor Courts dealt with those everyday
misdemeanours that affected the smooth running of the manor
or township. This was an ancient system that usefully kept anti-
social neighbours in check. It ensured that ditches were cleaned,
hedges pruned and animals were kept under control. The
practical management of a township and its tenants was carried
out by the bailiff of the lord of the manor, assisted by a jury
selected from the tenants, who served in turn. Anyone who failed
to turn up at court when required could be fined, as the courts
were an essential element in local order.

Some examples from the various local courts in the years
around 1700 show tenants neglecting to fill holes on Beam
Heath in Nantwich, taking sand from Willaston, taking clay from
Millstone Lane and not cleaning the brook leading from

Cheerbrook to Cheyney Brook. Richard Wright had broken open the gate of the local pound to take out his horse, which had been wandering round and impounded by the heathkeepers. In Barthomley residents were fined for not cleaning gutters, neglecting to mend sections of the lane, killing calves under age, felling trees without a licence, allowing cattle into the brook – and one character for using 'improbous' language. The most common problem in Monks Coppenhall was in fact the failure to clean the many ditches surrounding the fields, followed by not cropping over-hanging trees or cutting hedges and the township as whole was fined for not maintaining a section of the Valley Brook.

As for the criminal justice system, in the eighteenth century the attitude to crime in England changed and many more misdemeanours were liable to result in the death penalty. Power in Britain was now in the hands of the property owning classes and they were determined to protect their own interests by punishing those that threatened their material wealth. In the Assize Court, including that held in Hugh Lupus' hall in Chester Castle, many types of theft, such as pickpocketing items of over 1*s* value or stealing a sheep, were in theory, if not always in practice, capital offences. An increase in prosperity and commerce meant an increase in fraud and embezzlement, so forgery could also mean the gallows. In 1660 around 50 offences carried the death penalty; a century later the figure was 160, but in reality juries were often reluctant to convict and the courts often found ways of avoiding the ultimate penalty. Murder was frequently reduced to manslaughter and the guilty parties were branded, imprisoned with hard labour or, increasingly, transported.

Middlewich House of Correction in Dog Lane, now called Queen Street, opened in 1641, to reform criminals through hard labour and was the main institution of its type in the county. Elizabethan Poor Laws had originally intended such institutions to set the 'sturdy beggars' to useful work with some punishment in addition. Whippings were a common event, usually done publicly as evidenced by the cases of Richard and Samuel Williamson of Baddington, taylor and shoemaker, accused of petit larceny (theft of goods less than $12d$ in value). They were to be taken from Middlewich to Nantwich House of Correction, stripped naked from the waist up and given twenty-five lashes. Labourer Matthew Boyer of Nantwich was similarly convicted and was to be publicly whipped on the back of a cart in Nantwich for one hour from the bridge to the end of Pillory Street, after a spell of hard labour. Making oakum, picking old ropes into fibres to form caulking for waterproofing joints in boat building, was one of the jobs classified as hard labour. Margaret Taylor was also to be stripped naked from the waist up and whipped with twenty lashes at the public whipping post in Middlewich (the whipping of women was stopped by law in 1817). Some convicts were whipped at the end of every month of their sentence.

The replica stocks in Nantwich. (Susan Chambers)

In 1745 the keeper of Middlewich House of Correction came in for some criticism in a letter to the Justices in Quarter Sessions for his mild treatment of a prisoner by the name of James Strange, convicted of stealing leather. The 'Strange Gang', considered to be 'the most notorious that ever infested a town', were said to have insulted and laughed at the prosecution during their trial. However, the keeper, instead of making an example of Strange in a good public whipping, didn't notify any of the constables, and didn't take him to the Cross where the whipping was scheduled to start, and only gave him two or three gentle strokes with a whip made only of twine.

Little is know about the conditions in the House of Correction but accounts from the 1780s mention brooms for the cells, blankets and rugs, a tub for one of the dungeons, soap for the inmates' linen, clothing, 6lb of bread per week each and tobacco for them by order of the surgeon, though said to be for prevention of infection. Improvements were noted such as separation of males and females, access to water and in 1800 there are references to workrooms with looms, prisoners being employed in weaving, shoemaking, picking oakum and spinning jersey. A yard for female veteran offenders was available, with a 'dungeon or sleeping cell' with an iron-grated window and three bedsteads that could accommodate nine prisoners.

Many people, men and women, were sentenced to hang but subsequently had the punishment reduced to transportation to the colonies. The early transportees were shipped to America, usually Maryland, Virginia or to the West Indies, including Antigua, a 1718 Act standardising the process whereby vessel owners were paid for transporting the convicts. They were sentenced as indentured servants for seven or fourteen years and on arrival they would be auctioned like slaves. In 1736 a Nantwich man was packed off to the 'hulk' in the Mersey, an old vessel that was used temporarily to house the convicts prior to shipment to the American plantations. In 1775 the American War of Independence brought this to an end, and from 1787 convicts were taken to Australia, a journey of around three-and-a-half months.

The hulks were then used to house the rapidly growing number of convicts that the gaols could not cope with. In 1789 fourteen Cheshire prisoners were moved to them when gaol fever broke out amongst the eighty prisoners at the county gaol, parts of which had been demolished ready for re-building. When transportation to Australia began the hulks were used as temporary centres before the men were shipped off. The able-bodied convicts were often employed in the dock yards during the months when they were waiting for transportation. The *Justitia* hulks (there was a series of three of them), moored in the Thames off Woolwich, were the most notorious and sometimes residents awaiting passage to Australia included several men from the Crewe area. One of these was Basford poacher 20-year-old Thomas Lindop, found on Lord Crewe's land helping poacher Robert Baddiley (armed with a gun) and Ephraim Browne, a 51-year-old boatman from Minshull Vernon who had to leave his wife and five children behind in 1818 when he stole some malt from a boat. Salt was also a worthwhile product to steal as it could command a good price and there was plenty of it around in the area. James Rathbone, a 37-year-old salt boiler, was another local sent to the *Justitia* hulk on his way to Australia; he had taken 60lb of salt on three occasions from the salt works of Morris & Carter in Betchton. In 1826 30-year-old Samuel Nicklin, a labourer from Haslington, robbed Samuel Latham, landlord of the Cross Keys in Church Coppenhall, of two legs of pork (grand larceny), so he too was sent off to the hulk in the Thames before the longer journey to Australia.

A common crime locally was sheep stealing, for which the punishment theoretically was hanging, though it was usually reduced to transportation. James Cooper of Church Minshull went missing from his employer's land one day in 1830, together with a wether (a castrated ram), a ewe and a lamb. The farmer presumably initiated a countywide search, as the animals were found, recognisable by the owner's initials marked on them, a week later in a field belonging to a butcher in Alpraham. The farm hand, meanwhile, had joined the 3rd Regiment of Foot Guards and was hauled back from Windsor by the Nantwich constable. Another farm worker a few years later claimed to recognise the features of a lamb (though it had just been shorn) that he reckoned had been stolen from his brother-in-law in Hurleston. The case was marginally strengthened by the fact that the accused had been seen walking away from the field with a lamb on his back and that the lamb in question was obviously distressed and bleating for its mother. On this questionable evidence the prisoner was sentenced to death, though again the sentence was reduced. For stealing ducks two Nantwich men, John Bebbington and William Rixon, were given the option of six months' hard labour plus a public whipping on market day or entering the Navy. Bebbington died in prison before he could take up either option.

The stealing of grain was another common offence. In 1829 farmer Robert Pennell of Huntsbank Farm in Wistaston had his granary broken into and was robbed of farming tools and sacks of grain. In these days the elected local township constable was still the only law officer available to deal with such matters so many towns employed watchmen to keep an eye on things, and Nantwich was one such town. So apparently vigilant was this individual that on hearing noises in the house of one Samuel Williams, he gained access and found John Buckley, William Edwards and George Dunning with the bags of grain and farm tools. The accused and the grain were taken into custody, but Williams' wife took the opportunity to fling the farm implements into the nearby Weaver. The three robbers were at first sent to the *Gannymead* prison hulk on the Thames before transportation to Australia with ten other Cheshire men for seven years, and the receiver Williams for fourteen years.

In 1801 several women appeared at the Quarter Sessions, and all were being held in Middlewich House of Correction in

January that year. Mary Dunning, a 47-year-old weaver's wife had 'feloniously' milked several cows belonging to a Cholmondeston farmer, and had managed to make off with 6 quarts of milk. But 16-year-old Sarah White of Nantwich had been interested in different liquids – she had stolen a pint of rum, a pint of brandy and ale from William Mellor, publican. They were both let off relatively lightly with seven days imprisonment. Another Nantwich woman, Elizabeth Simmons, was charged with being a rogue and a vagabond, as she had been wandering in the town pretending to tell fortunes and practising various deceptions on his Majesty's subjects.

By 1811 Middlewich House of Correction was becoming very crowded and a decision was made to build a new prison at Knutsford, and work on this eventually commenced in 1817. By this time there was a particular problem with crime caused to a great extent by the vast number of men discharged from the Army at the end of the Napoleonic Wars with no employment to turn to. In 1843 Knutsford Gaol was the subject of an investigation by a Government inspector after allegations of gross mismanagement and corruption were made. Prisoners had been deprived of food, put to work in clearing sewage, forced to do housework for the officers and made to demonstrate the treadmill for the amusement of visitors.

There was a small house of correction with a workhouse built at Nantwich in 1677 on the site where the almshouses were built on Beam Street in 1767. Where the present Nantwich Museum stands on Pillory Street was a debtors' prison, the old Gaol House, with two dungeons. At one time this was in the possession of Lord Cholmondely, lord of the manor of the town and his lordship's bailiff was also the gaoler. By 1800 it was used to house a couple of lunatics, having taken in no debtors for twenty years.

Another gaol, known as the Round House (though it was rectangular), in Snow Hill, temporarily housed some notable prisoners in its time. It was a small building, very near the site of the present swimming pool, and had two damp dungeons, with small openings with iron gratings and its own stocks. In 1843 it accommodated Mary Gallop of Crewe, who was hanged at Chester for poisoning her father, and whose story is told in Chapter 7. The gaol also featured in the tale of the Darnhall Poachers, a gang of about twenty local men who were found poaching in Squire Corbett's Darnhall woods in December 1828. Having been spotted, the gang rashly fired at the keeper and another servant, and eventually made a successful getaway. The following February one of the gang was apprehended, eventually followed by the rest of them, and they were housed in the Round House whilst waiting trial. A crowd of local residents (perhaps a thousand or more according to reports) turned out to try and free them as they were being taken to a magistrate's hearing, forcing Major Tomkinson from Dorfold Hall to read the Riot Act ordering them to disperse, and troops were summoned from Chester to assist. At the trial seven of the men were sentenced to fourteen years transportation, and the rest imprisoned. However, a technical error was spotted on the indictment by a local solicitor, being the failure to state whether the event occurred after 12 midnight or midday. All the men were released after several months detention in the notorious hulk *Justitia*, where they were awaiting transportation. The Round House was demolished in 1848 and a police station was erected in its place.

In 1241 Welsh hostages were kept in Chester Castle and various parts of it were used as a gaol for the following six centuries. In the latter years of Elizabeth I's reign it housed a number of Catholic recusant prisoners and in 1715 around 500 Jacobite prisoners were lodged there. It later housed both debtors (for owing 40s or more) and people awaiting trial. The gaol was rebuilt in the late 1780s to a modern and enlightened design by Thomas Harrison, and as well as male and female cells, had day rooms, a laundry, a chapel, work rooms, an infirmary and convalescent rooms. Built of white stone, it was reported to be 'equal at least to any gaol in England', and 'remarkably clean'.

Chester city criminals were housed in the old Northgate Gaol in Chester, while those from the rest of the county were incarcerated in the Castle. All executions were actually arranged by the Sheriff of the city of Chester and carried out by his hangman in accordance with an ancient agreement. Until 1801 executions, including the occasional burning in the earlier days, were carried out at Boughton, a mile or so from the city centre. The final event at that site had been memorable, as one of the three felons took the opportunity to escape from the cart as it approached the spot, and tumbled down the bank into the River Dee and drowned, held under the water by his shackles. Another hanging later that year was the only one ever performed at the

Old Chester Castle, where for many centuries prisoners were incarcerated. (Cheshire Archives and Local Studies)

old Northgate Gaol. There were no hangings for the next eight years, and then in 1809 the new city gaol was used for another memorable execution when the ropes broke and a repeat performance had to be undertaken.

Hard labour at the county gaol was still a common sentence in the 1840s when James Creswell, 15, of Monks Coppenhall got six months labour for obtaining a pound of butter and two loaves by false pretences. And John Clayton had to labour hard there for eighteen months for stealing 10lb of bacon and 3lb of pig fat from a house in Haslington.

A serious increase in violence in the early years of the nineteenth century meant frequent calls on the regular military forces or the Cheshire Yeomanry for assistance. In the face of the inadequate capabilities of the voluntary township or parish constable in dealing with local crime, groups of village or townspeople began to organise themselves for this purpose from the latter years of the eighteenth century. In 1816 the Coppenhall Association for the Prosecution of Felons was formed by a dozen or so farmers, clergy and publicans in an attempt to prosecute some of the rogues who stole farm animals, timber, corn and so on. Members of the public who apprehended such villains would get a reward of 5 or 10 guineas. Any 'idle and disorderly vagrants' who ambled around the county without visible means of support were also to be brought to justice. Haslington had had such an association since 1782.

The nature of Coppenhall changed rapidly from the early 1840s when the town of Crewe was born in the new settlement created by the railway workshops that the Grand Junction Railway Company built there. The growing town had two railway company policemen by 1846, but this was still many years before a proper constabulary was established and petty crime was rife. Therefore, in 1844 the Coppenhall New Town Association was set up and advertised for members. It covered Wistaston, Minshull Vernon, Leighton, Willaston and adjoining areas and offered sums ranging from £21 for evidence towards a successful prosecution for murder, through stealing cheese, corn or milk from a cow, down to a 1 guinea reward for information concerning damage to fences and gates. Even the Grand Junction Railway Company became a member in an attempt to protect its estates and property in the new town.

Chapter 4

Hanged at Chester

In the decade before Victoria came to the throne several local men paid the ultimate price in a series of public executions in front of the City Gaol in Chester. The perpetrators of a spate of violent crimes had to be made examples of, claimed the Chief Justice in 1826, and John Green, 34, of Shavington, became one of those examples.

Samuel Dean, 65, and his wife lived in an isolated cottage at Bridgemere, on the London Road, about 1/2 mile north of the present garden centre. They had gone to bed before 10pm on 15 May 1826 with the door firmly barred and locked, but were woken with a start shortly after midnight by someone battering it down. Samuel climbed down the ladder from the bedroom to the living room and found two (or possibly three) men standing by the door. In the moonlight Samuel recognised one of them as John Green, a local young man who he had known for years. He was dressed in a velveteen jacket, which later helped to prove his identity, whilst the other man was wearing a traditional linen smock. The intruders claimed they wanted money and Green violently flung the old man into a chair in the living room, held him down and thrust a pistol into his chest demanding cooperation or 'I'll let light into you', and crushed his foot 'to a munch' by stamping on it.

Meanwhile, the other man, Green's brother-in-law 27-year-old Thomas Allmond, forced open a chest he had found in the parlour in which was about £17 and a lease. 'Give us two pounds of bacon and we'll go,' demanded Green when they had taken everything they wanted. The pair then made their escape, taking a basket of bits and pieces Mrs Dean had bought at Newcastle fair, goods from the dresser drawers and Dean's stockings, which he had left over the back of a chair. As they headed off in the moonlight Dean tried to pursue them down the lane but stopped to get help from neighbours, including a nearby farmer, and Tom Bankes. The latter, a former stonemason, was in fact Samuel's father-in-law, and had also been married to his sister for forty-one years. The lane was strewn with discarded clothing, shoes, caps and stockings.

The next day more of the booty was found further up the road towards Nantwich, including the pocket book that unbeknown to the robbers still had three £5 notes between its pages. As Dean claimed he recognised the intruders, he and some of his neighbours went with the local constable to the house near the main road in Shavington where Green lived with Allmond. They quickly uncovered evidence of the crime in the form of the old man's stockings hidden under leaves in a nearby ditch. Another indication of the guilt of the pair was the discovery of the stick that had been used to break open the chest and which had been left at the burgled cottage. It was recognised as one used for peeling bark as it left stains on the hands, and would have been a tool belonging to one of the men; they worked as leather tanners, a main source of employment in Nantwich. Green and Allmond were charged and tried for burglariously breaking into a dwelling house.

The men's wives were in fact sisters, and they all lived together. Green had married Elizabeth Delves in 1812 and by 1826 they had five children, the youngest being only 1 year old.

Green had little to say at his trial except that he had gone out to catch a rabbit for his wife who was very ill. He disputed that Samuel Dean could have recognised his voice as claimed because he probably hadn't heard him speak for fifteen years. Allmond had nothing to say at all. The men had apparently spent some time putting together an alibi, though the witnesses they produced made rather a poor job of telling their stories. A John Smith from Sandbach claimed he had visited the cottage with Mrs Green's brother, William Delves. He arrived before 10 pm after a walk of over 2 hours and found both the accused at the house just turning in for the night. Although the sleeping arrangements might appear somewhat unusual to our eyes, another visitor by the name of Pepper was sleeping with John Green, as Mrs Green was so ill she stayed up all night. Allmond was in bed with his wife and six children. Delves and Smith were certain they would have seen the accused going out. They claimed that they left at about 3 am, shaking hands with Green and Allmond (in their beds) on the way out. Delves was sure it was the night of 15 May when all of this happened, although he didn't know what day of the week it was.

The visitor called Pepper claimed he had gone to collect 11*s* owed to him by Green. He said he had been fed bacon and potatoes, actually shared a bed with the accused men and got up between 4 and 5 am and gone home. There were, he reckoned, four beds in the room, with him and the accused in one, Allmond's wife and children in another, a girl in the third with one of Green's daughters and the fourth bed empty.

Yet another version of events came from William Delves, Mrs Green's brother from Bilton. She had gone to bed at 10 pm with the nine children, and was so ill she had to be 'bolstered up'. He remembered that his father was also there, asleep upstairs and finally admitted to some confusion over the bed situation, but confirmed the accused were safe in bed at 3 am when he had bade them farewell. Only one of the beds was raised off the floor, he added. The township constable told the court that there were in fact only two beds and a ruck of straw, all in the one room.

The jury debated for 20 minutes and found Green guilty but acquitted Allmond. There had been a series of crimes of this type, and the judge chose to make an example of John Green by pronouncing the death penalty, with no option for transportation because of the seriousness of the case. He was hanged in Chester on 26 August 1826. Samuel Dean, the victim, went on to live to the ripe old age of 88.

'The Middlewich Gang' was a notorious bunch of robbers who were said to have terrorised the town in the late 1820s, some of whom ended their careers on the gallows. On Christmas Eve 1828 a Betchton farmer, Robert Mosley, had been to Sandbach market and had been enjoying several drinks before heading for home. He called into the Sandbach hostelries the George Inn and Thatched Tavern, then finally to the Crown just before 10pm, where he noticed three young men, James Harrop, John Proudlove and James Statham also having a few pints. Mosely eventually set off to walk the couple of miles home to Roughwood Farm, and had only gone a few hundred yards when in the moonlight he saw a man standing in the road. Feeling sociable after the few drinks he had consumed, he called

Old Middlewich. (Cheshire Archives and Local Studies)

a greeting but immediately received a blow on the head from behind. He was felled to the ground and pinned down by two men he later identified as James Harrop, 29, and John Proudlove, 25.

As the farmer struggled to get up, Harrop shouted 'Damn your blood, if you resist I'll knock your brains out' and smacked him down again. The third partner in the attack, James Statham, appeared from behind a hedge, rifled through his pockets and took the small amount of cash he found, whilst Proudlove took 10 sovereigns from the canvas purse that had attracted the attention of the gang when they were in the pub. The three of them then made their getaway towards Sandbach. The farmer continued home across the fields, got his manservant, a gun and a large dog and went back to see if he could find his money, but to no avail of course. At this time there was no fully functioning police force, and frequently the only assistance was from the elected constable, whose powers were very limited.

However, when the farmer was in Sandbach a few days after Christmas he spotted Harrop in the street, and then Proudlove at a pigeon shoot in the Red Lion and got the constable to arrest them. Their criminal careers came to an end when they were tried, together with Statham, the following April for aggravated highway robbery committed on Christmas Eve 1828 in Sandbach. Witnesses were produced who presented very unreliable alibis for Statham and Harrop, which the jury rejected, though Proudlove made no defence.

At the sentencing the judge donned the black cap and Proudlove spoke up to announce that he was alone at the scene of the crime. The judge told him he would make a public example of him, not so much for punishment of the individual but for the prevention of this sort of crime, whilst ridding the country of the other two by ordering life transportation.

Proudlove, whose mother was said to travel round selling items with a horse and cart, was formerly a shoe-maker and left a pregnant wife and two children. It seems surprising he hadn't

Sandbach Crosses, with the Crown in the background. Farmer Mosley enjoyed a Christmas Eve drink in this public house before he was attacked. (Cheshire Archives and Local Studies)

learned a lesson from his brother William's demise; William had been hanged in 1809 for shooting at an excise officer at Lawton Salt Works. He and his partner in crime, George Glover from Sandbach, had achieved unenviable fame by becoming known as 'the men they hanged twice'. The new 'drop' being used was a technical disaster when the ropes broke and the process had to be repeated an hour later. On 29 May, twenty years after his brother, John Proudlove was hanged, alongside John Leir, a fellow member of the 'Middlewich Gang'.

Leir, 21, was said to have had an excellent education and to be from a respectable Sandbach family. Nevertheless, he was involved in a brutal attack on an old man, a crime that caused widespread disgust in the area.

Retired clergyman the Revd Mathew Bloor, 80, lived in an isolated house in Stablach, about 2 miles from Middlewich, with some even older servants and a deaf and dumb woman. On the night of Saturday 14 March 1829 he was woken at about 1am by the sound of a door being forced open and then his bedroom door, though the latch was reinforced with an iron bar and a spade wedged against it, being broken down. He was violently beaten about the head and passed out. The men then rifled through the house, taking watches, silver spoons and money. John Foden, 87, one of the servants and nearly blind, went down the road sometime after 2 am to the house of farmer Benjamin Dobel, who returned with him. Finding the Revd Bloor bleeding heavily from his head injures, farmer Dobel said he thought he was dying. Whilst trying to make him comfortable, farmer Dobel found a lantern, probably a horn with a wick stuck in it, which contained a fragment of paper. This turned out to be part of a bill from a Middlewich grocer addressed to the wife of Sandbach man John Alcock.

The Revd Bloor soon claimed that he recognised one of the men who attacked him in his bedroom as Samuel Patterson, 26 and a local labourer. Suspicion also landed on a man named James Walker and consequently searches were carried out at his mother's property by the Middlewich constable. In the thatched roof of an outhouse the constable uncovered a stick with blood on one side and plaster on the other, said to be from the ceiling of the Revd Bloor's bedroom. Such had been the violence of the blows in the low-ceilinged room that the perpetrator appeared to have damaged it with the stick whilst battering the old man. A silver teaspoon with the initials S H was also found in a teapot in Walker's mother's house, Sarah Henshaw being the name of the elderly woman that lived at Bloor's house.

John Leir and John Bostock attempted to sell the stolen watch and some spoons (with the initials filed off) in Pendleton near Manchester. An observant constable nearby grew suspicious, searched the men and found the incriminating goods so they too were arrested.

Two brothers by the name of Alcock also fell under suspicion. They had been seen by a watchman at 5.40am, a few hours after the attack, on the road from Stablach. In addition, there was the question of the piece of paper with Alcock's name on it found at the scene of the crime, though there was a query as to whether the grocer's bill of which this was a fragment had ever been delivered to him.

At the trial it was reported that Leir and one of the Alcocks had been seen drinking in the Paul Pry pub in Wheelock Street, Middlewich, on the night of the attack. Another publican, Robert Lightfoot of Winsford, whose pub was about 6 miles from Bloor's house, gave an alibi for one of the men and probably saved him from the gallows. He said that Walker had been drinking in his pub till late on the Saturday night, hours before the robbery, and left carrying a drunken man on his back at nearly midnight. That drunk, William Banks, claimed that several men including Walker had gone to 'the salt-house' when they left the pub as he couldn't go any further. This alibi protected Walker as the verdict was that Patterson and Leir were guilty, the others not guilty. As the black-capped judge sentenced them to be hanged by the neck, Leir proclaimed himself innocent, and Patterson, having been apparently unconcerned up to this point, said to Leir 'Now tell it all, you know I'm innocent'.

Leir did not oblige but a royal pardon was suddenly granted to Patterson a week before he was due to hang as he managed to prove he had been elsewhere (possibly committing another crime). The Revd Bloor was apparently mistaken when he identified Patterson, and whoever it was that had attacked him was never discovered. Leir, a former silk worker at John Bull & Co.,

Sandbach was hanged, the same day as fellow gang member John Proudlove, and their bodies returned to Sandbach for burial.

'The Bloody Assize' was the term used to describe a series of cases in spring 1834 that led to five men being condemned to hang. One of them was John Carr, 27, a tall good-looking man tried for feloniously and maliciously cutting and wounding Thomas Horton at Haslington.

The scene of the crime was a yard at the back of a Haslington pub, the Fox. On the night of 25 October 1833 Carr approached Horton and asked for return of 2*d* which he'd been owed for a couple of years. Horton said he'd have to wait as he didn't have change for a shilling. Carr eventually left the pub for half an hour or so, but returned in a fighting mood, battering on the pub door and threatening to kill or spoil the first man that came through it. Horton went out 'for some purpose' through the back door of the pub and Carr followed him and launched an attack with a knife, knocking him down and stabbing him in the back near his kidney, and cutting his head resembling 'the superficial cuts on roasted pork'. Horton had twenty separate injuries on his head, neck, loins, back and sides, with damage to arteries involved, and was lucky to escape with his life.

The jury returned a guilty verdict and the judge said it was obvious that Carr had intended murder. He deplored the fashion for carrying knives and decided to make an example of Carr by sentencing him to death. In the days leading up to the execution four condemned men lodged in the county gaol in Chester Castle were visited regularly by the Chaplain, and treated to a sermon in the chapel on 'The wages of sin is death'. The actual execution site was the city gaol on the plot of the present Queens School, and the prisoners were taken there, accompanied by a vast crowd, soon after 5 am. They continued to pray with the chaplains and a hymn was sung. In his final hours a penitent Carr professed to having once been a member of the Primitive Methodists but admitted he had lapsed and resorted to frequent drunkenness. In fact, he claimed he had been so drunk when he committed the attack that he hadn't realised what he had done until his wife told him. The men were hanged at 1.30pm, and Carr's body was buried in the churchyard of St Mary's, next to Chester Castle.

Chapter 5

Poachers and Robbers

The Grand Junction Railway Company's new line through Monks Coppenhall was completed and opened for traffic in 1837. The first houses for the workers at the new railway company workshops were ready for occupation six years later, and the town's population began its meteoric rise from a couple of hundred to thousands.

Life carried on as normal in the towns and villages of south-east Cheshire, as did the criminals. There were, as always, a number of people who stole the essentials of life like food in various shapes and forms. A couple of boys from Nantwich were given a month's hard labour for stealing apples from a cart, possibly putting them off apples for life. James Tomlinson and Charles Palin of Warmingham stole four bushells of potatoes from Thomas Hall, who had the farm on Drury Lane where the house called The Meadows now stands.

Ducks and geese were also a popular target and Thomas and William Evans, boatmen, were charged with stealing three geese from Thomas Done of Cholmondeston a week before Christmas. They broke into the geese pen in the dark, leaving a trail of footprints and feathers back to where their boat had been, so a constable followed the boat, and found them cooking a goose. Poor Thomas, whose footprints matched the evidence, paid with twelve months' hard labour.

A similar story of indisputable evidence concerned the theft of a sheep from Hooter Hall Farm in Haslington, which in 1837 was the home of cheese factor John Elliot. The sheep was a wether and had a bell round its neck so that the flock could be tracked down as they would follow the 'bell wether'. One morning one of Elliot's servants found the wether gone, but a pile of sheep entrails in a sandpit in the same field. Luckily the servant had his suspicions and a constable was sent to the Wheelock cottage of John Harrison, where he found a sheep's head and feet, a carcase and a bell. The judge, in summing up, told the jury that there was a problem with the indictment in that Harrison should have been charged with killing the sheep with intent to steal part of it, rather than stealing the sheep. However, there was also a count on the indictment charging him with stealing the bell, which was larceny, so he could be convicted on that count. So he was transported for seven years for stealing the bell.

Randle Clark, labourer, had stolen 50lb of coal worth 6*d* from a boat on the canal at Elton, for which he got three months' hard labour. The same applied to Thomas Condliffe who stole a batten of straw from William Morris of Arclid valued at 2*d*. Samuel Bostock, 18, of Minshull Vernon was charged with stealing such articles as a tail puller, a plashing hook, a horse brush, a cart whip, a wire wheat riddle and a cart whip, for which he was transported for seven years and one day. Pigeon rearing and breeding was a popular hobby and a good specimen could command a reasonable sum. Did Thomas Dale of Nantwich think the three pigeons he stole were worth his nine months' hard labour?

Poaching at this time was rife, and occasionally a night spent shooting the local landowner's game would end in tragedy. In 1843 four men from Wettenhall, William Warburton, Samuel Cousins, Richard Evans and Joseph 'Duke' Baker (though he had so far avoided apprehension), were charged with having been out in unlawful pursuit of game one night the previous October. On the night in question a gamekeeper, Richard Chesters, had been killed, though for some mysterious reason on which the attorney general declined to elaborate there would not be a capital charge.

Word had gone round that a poaching party would be out in Wettenhall woods on the night of 22 October, so a strong contingent of local gamekeepers were called up for duty. Robert Bostock, the keeper for Edwin Corbett of Darnhall, his wagoner John Noden, Daniel Bebbington, keeper of Wettenhall wood for John Tollemache, John Bebbington, Corbett's under-keeper, and Richard Chesters, assistant keeper, were all ready for action in the woods that night. Part of the wood was a new plantation known by the strange name of Boffey's Pipe, and a field belonging to John Boffey (who farmed at what is now Village Farm) lay next to it. It was a moonlit night and as the keepers arrived they immediately spotted the group of four men at the edge of the Pipe. Three of the men had guns, and one had what was termed a 'bludgeon', a weapon a yard long, 3 or 4in thick,

The injured gamekeeper was taken to the Boot and Slipper Inn in Wettenhall, seen here in a late eighteenth-century drawing. (Cheshire Archives and Local Studies)

South View of the Buildings on Oulton's Tenement.

with a wrist string. The guns were pointed at the keepers but they nevertheless continued to advance until they were right in front of the poachers, who were standing their ground so a dangerous situation was developing.

John Bebbington, who features in another poaching tragedy later in this book, bravely seized the muzzle of one of the guns, despite being struck on the head by the poachers. The gun went off, but he managed to wrestle its owner to the ground and left him in the charge of Daniel Bebbington. Meanwhile, Bebbington set off after John 'Duke' Baker, catching him in the Pipe, aided by Richard Chesters. There was some confusion in the darkness when the other poachers approached, calling, 'How are you getting on?', which was mistaken for the keepers by John Bebbington who replied, 'We're here!' At this point the poachers took the initiative and began assaulting the keepers with guns and the bludgeon, stunning them, and knocking one of them into the brook. As the keepers began to gather their wits, they found Chesters lying nearby obviously badly injured, and one of them ran to the Boot and Slipper Inn in Wettenhall for help.

The injured keeper was carried unconscious to the inn and a surgeon called from Tarporley, who bled him with leeches but to no avail. There was bleeding under his scalp and from his right ear, and he died within hours. An inquest found that he had several skull fractures but no gunshot wounds. Suspects were brought in and charged. Some neighbours attempted to provide alibis at the trial, and the defence argued that the indictment was suspect because of a technicality as to whether Boffey's Pipe was part of Wettenhall wood.

The judge sentenced the men to eighteen months' imprisonment, rather than transportation, as he said it was not clear who had been responsible for the death of Chesters. The sentence was reduced by five months as they had already been in custody for this length of time. It has to be said they appear to have got off relatively lightly in this instance.

Highway robbery was frequent, though it was usually a more mundane process than a masked man on horseback flourishing a pistol. It was much more akin to what we might call 'mugging' nowadays. In 1841 a group of men were going home from Nantwich fair in the early evening and were attacked by William Heath, who knocked one of the party down, hit another one around the head and took a purse from his breeches pocket. He was thwarted by the group yelling 'Murder', and at his trial was lucky to get away with a charge of assault (two months' hard labour) rather than robbery.

A couple of months later a woman also on her way home from Nantwich fair was robbed and five people were indicted. Margaret Donnelly was on her way back to Newcastle when she was knocked down and her pockets containing 15*s* were ripped off. She identified the assailants to the constable in a public house back in Nantwich, but fearing a revenge attack refused to give evidence and they were discharged.

She was actually proved right in her fears, when she was assaulted in the course of what the defence lawyer described as no more than an Irish pot-house row. Margaret said she was lodging at Sandbach and was drinking gin and peppermint in a spirit vault when two women came into the room and attacked her crying, 'You bloody . . ., I'll have your life now'. The landlord separated the fighting women and Margaret ran to her lodgings and locked herself in, but one of the women and two men broke in and beat the poor woman with a poker and slashed her with a knife. At the subsequent trial Margaret revealed that she had on several occasions been threatened by the gang for giving information about them concerning the robbery. One of the women charged, Ann Williams, claimed that the other accused, Phoebe Cook, had been beaten by the man that Margaret Donnelly lived with, and that he had given Ann a black eye when she challenged him about it. The jury had little sympathy with Margaret and returned a not-guilty verdict.

Sandbach Market in earlier times. (Cheshire Archives and Local Studies)

On 18 July 1837, two weeks after the opening of the new railway, Boswell Meredith, a 69-year-old farmer who lived near the corner of Colleys Lane in Willaston, was the victim of a vicious attack. The three assailants were brothers John Steele, a pottery worker, and George Steele, a labourer, and Benjamin Webb, a collier. The trio were reputedly part of a well-known gang of ruffians. They were lodging in Tunstall, Staffordshire, and as it was Tunstall wakes week and there was little work to be had the three men had come by foot into Cheshire. They were planning on doing a bit of mowing in the Hough for the Steeles' father, who ran the farm that is now called Ellesmere Farm, but the weather turned out to be too wet and they had to change their plans. They had been hanging around the area all day, spending a couple of hours in the afternoon in the Rockwood public house, drinking and eating bread and cheese. They were spotted walking past the smithy on Crewe Road (where Smithy House Farm now stands) in the direction of Colleys Lane at about 4 pm, obviously at a loose end and with a few pints of beer working its mischief. John Steele had said to the other two that there was a man living nearby to whom he owed a grudge, and he intended to settle it.

Boswell Meredith was the unfortunate victim of the grudge, and as it was still raining the trio settled down in his barn. They slept for several hours, and also passed the time by cutting the handles off a couple of rakes and pitchforks for use as weapons. At around 11 pm they began to put their plan into action. One of the gang roused Mr and Mrs Meredith from their sleep by shouting from their garden and saying that their cattle had got into a neighbour's field of potatoes and were damaging the plants. The old man put on some clothes and hurried outside to retrieve his cows whereupon the trio launched a vicious attack with their home-made weapons. They left him badly injured around the head and arms in a ditch full of water. He eventually managed to drag himself to another farm nearby where his cries were heard by John Wilkinson, the occupant of a house down Colleys Lane, who helped the wounded farmer back to his house where his wife Mary was waiting. He had serious head injuries and was unable to speak coherently, so at about 6.30am she called the doctor, Dr Brady from Nantwich. Unfortunately, he could do nothing and the farmer died two days later from a fractured skull.

John Meredith, the farmer's son, arrived from his farm, Sound Hall, a few miles away and found footprints in the yard. The Nantwich constable conscientiously measured and covered these with a board to preserve then as evidence before managing to follow the tracks about half a mile towards the Hough.

Mr Meredith junior also offered a £100 reward for

information and that same day John Steele was reported as having blood on his clothes and was arrested by his local constable. The other two gave themselves up and all three began blaming each other for the attack. Webb claimed that the shoes that matched the footprints had been worn originally on the night by him, but then by John Steele, and they had changed shoes near Crewe Gates. John Steele said the blood on his coat had been there for three weeks since he'd been involved in a fight. He then claimed to have only struck Meredith with his hand and to have been chased off by a dog, though Webb said the brothers had been beating the old man with the sticks. George Steele said John had struck him with his hand, and then Webb had hit him with a stick saying he'd quieten him down.

The judge advised the jury to deliberate carefully, and bear in mind that there had been no deadly weapons such as knives or daggers used, so had the men actually meant to commit murder? The jury obviously thought not as they returned verdicts of manslaughter. The judge congratulated them on their decisions and their merciful view of the case and announced sentences of transportation for life. At this point Webb informed a constable that as George Steele had given evidence against him he would reveal where property stolen by Steele in the Potteries could be found.

Skerrat and Remer was a firm of solicitors in Sandbach in the early 1840s, and employed three clerks to deal with large amounts of money that passed through the office. One Friday night in January 1841 about £1,100 had been left in an iron safe, consisting of Bank of England notes (in £100, £50, £20 and £5 denominations), local notes and bank post bills. At this time notes were still issued by many different local banks. On the following Saturday morning one of the clerks turned up for work and discovered the outside door had been forced, the iron safe broken into and the money taken.

On that same Saturday morning two men, James and Thomas Hampton, went into a haberdashery shop in Tunstall, about

9 miles from Sandbach, run by George Edwards. The two men tried to buy a shawl for 9*s*, for which was offered a Lane End £5 note and change including 4 sovereigns given. Lane End was a small town in the Potteries, now known as Longton, and may well have been home to the bank issuing Lane End banknotes. One of the men tried to buy some cord and offered an Imperial Bank note. George Edwards was obviously suspicious and took it to a solicitor, who directed him to take it to Mr Remer, as the note was from a bank that had closed and so was of no value. The Hampton brothers made further attempts to use the Imperial Bank notes but met with little success as traders were wary of them. They'd gone to buy some alcohol and Thomas Hampton had started flashing sovereigns around saying, 'I can buy you and your house and all the things in it'. A couple of days later they went back to the same place and again attempted to use the Imperial Bank notes, but still with no joy.

The brothers were beginning to look suspicious and were attracting attention so five days after the robbery a Congleton constable searched their home and found the shawl they'd bought. James Hampton's footprints were compared with the impressions that a Sandbach police officer had taken outside the burgled premises and they matched. They were soon tried and found guilty, and then appeared on another charge of burglary in Tunstall. Transportation for a total of fourteen years was imposed on the two brothers.

In the nineteenth century elections aroused much more interest and excitement than they do nowadays. In 1841 in Nantwich there was a riot and a man was killed after being pelted with stones and falling from a coach which was conveying voters who favoured Tollemache and Egerton (the South Cheshire Tory candidates) from the poll in the Union Inn. The coachman was attacked with mud and bricks and was stunned by a blow from a stone thrown by Michael Byrne, who was consequently charged with riot and assault. In the course of the day a magistrate had to read the Riot Act, which signified that if the crowd failed to disperse within an hour force would be used on them. A peace officer slashed to bits an effigy that had been thrown into the face of a horse.

The defence at the trial was that this was a political prosecution, and that if the death that occurred could be blamed on anything it was the use of the military and the arming of peace officers with swords. The judge gave Byrne twelve months and some other rioters six months. John Tollemache, the largest landowner in Cheshire at the time, was elected MP and retained office for twenty-seven years. He built the imposing Peckforton Castle for himself in 1844.

Chapter 6

The Ritual Drowning of Sarah Cartwright

On Saturday, 2 December 1843, the Grand Junction Railway Company (GJR) organised a dinner and a display of fireworks in Monks Coppenhall to celebrate the opening of their locomotive works. Repair sheds for the Company had formerly been at Edgehill, Liverpool, until March 1843, when the all the work and employees were transferred to this remote, rural parish in south Cheshire. Even before the inhabitants had moved in, the directors of the GJR called this embryonic new town Crewe. At least three people from this young community were prevented from participating in the revelry and celebrations that marked the opening of the works. Sarah Cartwright, one of the few pregnant ladies in the new town, was dead, having been drowned just over a week before. Her husband, Thomas, and a work colleague, Jonathan Pogmore, were on remand at Chester, charged with causing her death. All three were members of the Mormon church in the town, though, as it will be seen, Sarah was a reluctant convert.

Most of the workmen who were transferred from Liverpool to the Monks Coppenhall Works brought their families, furniture and religious beliefs with them. Within a year of the transfer, Anglicans, Baptists, three types of Methodists, Presbyterians, Welsh Calvinists, Roman Catholics and Congregationalists had organised regular services, in addition to the Mormons, or Church of the Latter-Day Saints as they preferred to be called. As we shall see, the death of Sarah Cartwright was to blank out

One night in November 1843 Sarah Cartwright was swept along this stretch of the Valley Brook. The line of the watercourse was straightened many years ago. (Peter Ollerhead)

the early Mormon presence in Crewe, leaving all of the other religious denominations to forge ahead without them.

Thomas Cartwright, aged 29, was a blacksmith who worked in the GJR forge, a few yards from the door of his recently built cottage. His 30-year-old wife Sarah was expecting their fourth child in the early months of 1844, and was, no doubt, looking forward to celebrating Christmas in this unfamiliar region, with, perhaps, a visit to their relatives in the Lancashire seaport. Other matters intervened, however, when Thomas was converted to the Mormon faith as a result of the militant ministration of Jonathan Pogmore, his foreman in the forge. The Cartwrights, like all of the migrants from Liverpool, had to establish new friends and relationships, having been uprooted from a familiar neighbourhood to be planted in a small urban colony in a rural setting. As a result, Thomas Cartwright eagerly embraced the friendship, and teachings, of his immediate boss, and the intimate fellowship of the small Mormon community.

Jonathan Pogmore (or Pugmire in Mormon records) was born at Castle Sowerby, Cumberland, in the last year of the eighteenth century. As an experienced blacksmith, he easily obtained employment in the GJR workshops at Edgehill, Liverpool, in the late 1830s. At this time the first Mormon missionaries landed there, from the USA. Within 4 years, they had over 4,000 converts in Liverpool, and the surrounding counties. Amongst these newly introduced members of the Latter-Day Saints were Jonathan Pogmore and his wife Elizabeth, who were both baptised by immersion in the River Mersey.

On relocating to the railway colony at the new Crewe, in 1843, Pogmore continued as foremen over the blacksmiths, whose number included Thomas Cartwright. About eight months after his arrival, Thomas was baptised by Jonathan Pogmore, now the Elder of the small Mormon church, on 6 November in the Valley Brook. Suspecting such an event was imminent, the antagonistic Sarah searched the streets of the small colony only to find him, and the baptismal party, returning along the rough road between Oak Farm and the railway cottages. She upbraided her husband with a series of oaths, also including members of the Pogmore family in her invective.

Despite his wife's negative attitude towards the Mormon Church, Thomas continued to attend the Pogmore home, for prayer and teaching, while at the same time seeking to indoctrinate his wife with his newly acquired faith. It must be remembered that only one of the Christian groups (the Wesleyan

Association Methodists) had a chapel at this point in time. None of the others had separate premises for worship, so they had to meet in cottages, or similar venues, excepting the Anglicans, who were allowed the use of a room in the GJR works. Eventually, and only after much pressure, Sarah reluctantly agreed, on 23 November, to be baptised by Elder Jonathan Pogmore, as a sign of her conversion to the Mormon faith. So, before she could change her mind, Thomas Cartwright rapidly arranged for the baptism to take place that very evening, in the Valley Brook or River Waldron, the main watercourse of the parish that was also used for baptismal purposes, by Alan Priest and the few local Baptists that he led.

Over the years, this stream had cut a steep valley through the heavy clay, forming the main topographical feature in the parish. It also provided the thousands of gallons of water a day that were needed for GJR works and homes, as well as being the town's conduit for sewage and waste water at that stage in its development. A reservoir, between the works and the station, had been constructed by the GJR, to allow the water to be pumped by a steam engine to a filtering tank. Normally, the brook, which rises in the hills near to Talke in Staffordshire, was a pleasant stream that meandered 15 miles or so through the pasture land of south Cheshire until it joined the River Weaver.

Thomas Cartwright called at the house of a Mr Hulme, who had joined the Mormons a week or so earlier, requesting him to witness the baptism, and for Mrs Hulme to look after the three Cartwright children. After prayer at the Pogmore house, Thomas and Sarah, along with a small party of Mormons, walked in the darkness, crossing the Chester line, into the present High Street, reaching the Valley Brook, where previous baptisms had taken place. Altogether, it was a journey of only a few hundred yards. Unfortunately, conditions were not the same as on other occasions, as the day had been very stormy, with torrential rain, meaning that the brook was in flood and the bank leading down to it was treacherous and slippery.

By the light of the stars, Sarah Cartwright, who was six months pregnant, was completely disrobed by Elizabeth Pogmore, and then dressed in a flannel shirt of her husband's, which only reached to her waist. Without the benefit of a lantern, the party examined a stretch of the brook to the west of what is now Mill Street, declaring it safe to proceed with the rite; they could not use the familiar spot on account of the increased depth of the water. Standing near to the bank of the flowing stream, the Mormon elder called for Sarah to make her way to him. Holding her by the hands, with one arm under her back, he laid her backwards into the full spate of the stream, to complete the ritual.

Whether through the shock of the cold water or the strength of the torrent, she began to struggle, slipping from his grasp to be taken down stream, by the swirling undercurrent. Pogmore also stumbled at the same time and was only saved when James Moore, one of the Morman witnesses, quickly grabbed him, and with the assistance of Elizabeth Pogmore, pulled him up out of the swollen stream and onto the bank. Cartwright, meanwhile, had jumped in to try to save his drowning wife, but was unable to locate her, despite swimming, or being swept, a hundred yards or so down stream. Hulme and another GJR workman, George Knowlen, ran up and down frantically searching for any sign of Sarah, only to find Cartwright desperately holding onto a tree stump. Together, they pulled him out of the sullen waters, to the safety of the fields of Oak Farm.

After a further fruitless search for Sarah Cartwright, the depleted and wet baptismal party dejectedly returned to their homes in the railway village. Within a short time, the dreadful news reached the Revd J Appleton, the resident Anglican clergyman at the new Crewe, who arranged for the magistrates to institute an inquiry, after placing Pogmore into the custody of the parish constable. (The Mormon record states that Pogmore was dragged by the authorities from the arms of his family.) Cartwright was arraigned alongside him, after attending his wife's burial in St Michael's churchyard, at Church Coppenhall, detailed in the parish register as taking place on 26 November through being 'drowned by Mormonite immersion'.

On the morning following the disaster, a search was made of the area. A George Bazeley found the body of Sarah some 300yd to the west of where she had entered the stream. By this time, the water had subsided to such a degree that her corpse was caught in undergrowth, about 8ft from the stream. Michael Kinty, a representative of the civil power, was taken to view the baptismal spot. Here the brook, instead of its usual depth of 2ft, was, even then, some 16 hours after the tragic event, still 6ft deep, having fallen some 3ft during the night.

The fitting shop in Crewe works at the end of 1843. (Peter Ollerhead)

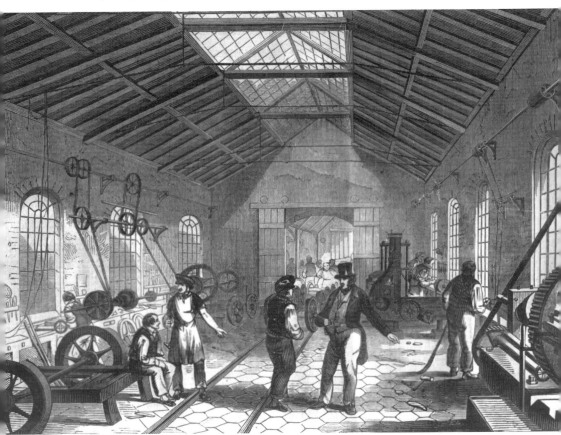

A few days later, an inquest was held at the Adelphi Hotel, in what is now Market Street, before Mr Roscoe, the district coroner. Having patiently listened to all the facts, a jury brought in a verdict of manslaughter against both Pogmore and Cartwright. After being officially charged with causing the death of Sarah Cartwright, they were remanded to Chester Castle, an action that meant Cartwright celebrated his thirtieth birthday, as well as Christmas Day, in prison.

On Thursday, 4 January 1844, the Assize Court was convened at Chester, under Mr Justice Wightman. The first case to be tried was that of Jonathan Pogmore, blacksmith and officiating minister of the Crewe Mormons, and Thomas Henry Cartwright, who were both placed at the bar charged with killing and slaying Sarah Cartwright at Monks Coppenhall. According to *The Times*, the prisoners were 'decently attired presenting the ordinary appearance of respectable mechanics', which is exactly what they were.

Opening the case for the prosecution, the Attorney General for Cheshire stated that the prisoners were indicted for the killing, but whether from premeditation or negligence was for the jury to decide. Unfortunately, the jury was deliberately prevented from arriving at a just decision owing to the non-appearance of the witnesses. As the baptism had been arranged at short notice, on a very dark and stormy night, the only witnesses to the event were especially invited loyal members of the local Mormon church. Other persons who were involved in the later search, such as George Bazeley and Lucy Massey, did answer their call. The latter, a neighbour of Sarah's, testified that she was in good health when they talked together, for about 10 minutes, on the day of the baptism, which was, of course, the day of her death.

When a lawyer, named Temple, engaged by the Mormons, cross-examined Bazeley for the defence, he seemed to be seeking a justification from Scripture for baptisms being conducted in a river and in the open air. The witness was unable to help in this, as he stated that he had never seen the River Jordan nor visited the Holy Land, though he was able to confirm that the spot where Sarah met her death was usually very pleasant and tranquil.

When James Moore, and other Mormons, were called by the usher to give their testimony of the tragic event, they purposefully absented themselves, to ensure that their fellow sectarians were not convicted, an action that made the judge livid. Consequently, as the material facts regarding the calamitous baptism could not be substantiated, Mr Justice Wightman had no alternative than to direct the jury to return a not-guilty verdict, though he ordered that every Mormon witness should forfeit his recognisance. In his later selective record of the drowning, and its consequences, Jonathan Pogmore junior, who was 20 at the time of the incident, wrote that the judge advised the jury to be very careful when considering the facts of the case, as it involved almighty God and those that worshipped Him. This is not a true view of the judge's attitude, as presented by contemporary accounts of the trial that were published in newspapers of the time.

On their release, Cartwright and Pogmore went home to the mechanics' colony at Monks Coppenhall only to find that they, and all the other Mormons working for the Grand Junction Railway in the new Crewe, had no jobs. At a board meeting on 7 February 1844, the GJR directors ratified the action of the local management of the Crewe workshops, who discharged all those who would not cooperate with the civil power. The minute of 7 February stated that:

> *the Mormon workmen who refused to attend the*
> *trial thereby defeating the ends of justice . . . be no*
> *longer retained in the service of the Company.*

That action removed the Mormon presence from the town for more than a hundred years. As Crewe was a single-industry town, it meant there was no alternative employment for them, other than the railway.

Jonathan Pogmore, along with his wife Elizabeth and 6 of their 7 children, decided to join the stream of migrants sailing from Liverpool to the USA, amounting to a tiny fraction of the 66,584 who left Liverpool that year. These migrants, in the middle years of the nineteenth century, formed what was a massive relocation of the poor and destitute, mainly from Ireland, to a better life in the New World. Between 1840 and 1849, nearly 2 million people left the shores of Great Britain to travel westwards to North America.

The Pogmores sailed from Liverpool to New Orleans on board the packet ship *Isaac Allerton* on 11 February 1844, a voyage that lasted 45 days. From New Orleans they travelled up the Mississippi on a steamboat to Nauvoo, Illinois, from where they removed to Iowa and then to Nebraska. During the extremely harsh winter of that year Elizabeth Pogmore died, along with hundreds of other settlers. The following spring, Jonathan, who had quickly remarried, joined in a covered wagon journey overland to Salt Lake City, Utah, where he is commemorated on a plaque to this day. He died of inflammation of the lungs, aged 77, on 9 August 1876.

After his release from Chester Castle, Thomas Cartwright returned to Lancashire with his three children, Jane aged 7, Sarah (4) and Ellen (2). Within six months he was married to Jane Allen, a 26-year-old from Dublin who had migrated to Liverpool, where she soon became a Mormon after renouncing her native Catholicism. Retaining his Mormon faith, in 1848 Cartwright sailed to the USA, with Sarah and Ellen, from his first marriage, and two young children from his second. A further four children were born in the USA, one, Caroline, on a riverboat. Making their way to Utah, the couple lived in Beaver, where Thomas earned his living as a blacksmith. Sometime during these years, Thomas took Catherine Beswick as an additional wife, a custom that was allowed under Mormon doctrines. They all lived together happily, or otherwise, until Thomas died in 1872. He was laid to rest in the Mormon cemetery at Beaver, Utah, and a long way from Upholland, near to Wigan, where he had been born.

The two Liverpool-born children of Sarah Cartwright who emigrated to the USA with their father and his new bride in 1848 embraced the Mormon faith when they came of age. Ellen was married in 1860 and was delivered of thirteen children before she died in 1928, aged 86. Sarah did not live as long, though before she died, in 1885, she had provided her father with five grandchildren. She was buried at Hyrum in Utah.

For a number of years the stretch of the River Waldron between Mill Street and Edleston Road in Crewe was known as 'Sally's Valley', as recorded in the Revd G Pegler's article *The Waters of Crewe*, published in 1914. 'Sally's Valley' was so named in memory of an old woman accidentally drowned there many years before. While the Revd Pegler got some of the facts wrong, even this brief reference has now disappeared from the collective memory of the town. So ends the story of Sarah Cartwright, of Liverpool, who moved to a new life in Monks Coppenhall only for it to be ended with lamentable suddenness on a dark and stormy night in November 1843.

Chapter 7

The Tragedy of Mary Gallop

Neat rows of new houses greeted the workers moving from the grimy bustle of Liverpool into the new railway colony at Crewe in 1843. Most of the cottages had porches and little gardens, many had gas and running water and the streets were wide. There were already a few shops, a school, assembly rooms, a surgery and plans for a church. However, the uprooted families did not always find a happy new life awaiting them.

The Gallop family came from Upper Stanhope Street in Toxteth Park. Richard Gallop was a joiner married to his second wife Mary, who was twenty years his senior. They were accompanied by their daughters, the younger one also called Mary, who was 19, and Margaret, a daughter of Richard's first marriage. They had lived just over a mile away from the Edgehill railway workshops that were being moved to the new site in Crewe. The family had already moved around, having earlier lived in Warrington, where young Mary was born in March 1824, Runcorn and other parts of Liverpool. As they settled into one of the new houses in Crewe, they must have found it quite a contrast to the home they had left. Beyond the bounds of the Grand Junction Railway's estate there was still nothing but open fields and a few scattered cottages. The market town of Nantwich was at least an hour's walk away up Mill Lane, past the new flour mill on the Valley Brook and Dairy House Farm at the top of the lane on the corner of the turnpike road.

The 1843 celebrations held to mark the opening of Crewe Railway Works.
(Peter Ollerhead)

For several years young Mary had been friendly with a boy from Edgehill, a bit younger than herself, though her parents, particularly her father, did not approve of the relationship. When Mary and her mother went back to their old Liverpool home for a visit after about three months in Crewe, she saw the young man, who was an apprentice, several times and they began to write to each other; Mary used to show the letters to her mother but not her father.

The Gallops were strong Wesleyan Methodists like a lot of the Crewe incomers and Mary was a Sunday school teacher in the new town, her only other occupation being keeping house for the family. Like many households, they had taken a lodger, William

Frazer, a coach-body maker, to help with the finances. In addition, as a sideline, Richard Gallop made plasters for cuts and bruises and dabbled in producing medicines, which he gave to the men in the railway works. He was said to have given Nathaniel Worsdell, coaching superintendent of the Grand Junction Railway, some logwood for a bowel complaint.

In April 1844, ten months after coming to Crewe, Mary Gallop senior killed herself, obviously a traumatic event for the young Mary who it was said did not sleep for a week afterwards. She discovered the body of her mother, with her throat cut, one morning when she got up, after her father had gone to work. The death certificate stated: 'Cut her throat being lunatic'. It was reported at the inquest into her death that she had acted very strangely whilst pregnant with Mary; she had at one time deliberately set fire to the bed, and had frequently gone out with the intention of drowning herself. After the funeral Mary and her half-sister went to stay near their former home in Edgehill for a while, and Mary continued her friendship with the young man. In late October Mary asked her father about the possibility of going to see her friend at Christmas, but he would not entertain the idea at all, became very angry and said he would never let Mary have anything to do with the youth. After a row about some over-cooked potatoes, he threatened to beat her with his strap. At this point Mary considered leaving the family and working as a servant in Liverpool, but unfortunately did not pursue the scheme.

Instead, an idea was put into her head by her half-sister, who casually mentioned someone who had poisoned her husband with arsenic. The wife, it was said, had bought arsenic on the pretence of it being for rat poison. The thought of being rid of her father and being able to go where she wanted was planted and it flourished, and this fatal scheme resulted in his death on Sunday, 3 November.

Richard Gallop had been complaining of bowel problems for some weeks and frequently took arrowroot mixed with milk and sugar. It acted as a thickening agent and was considered to be of nutritional benefit when people were sick. In fact, arrowroot with pomegranate was sometimes prescribed by one of the local druggists. Mary bought her arrowroot from a Crewe shop run by Mr Pickersgill, druggist and grocer. Very conveniently mice and possibly even rats had been seen in the house despite the fact that it was almost brand new. This made things a little easier for Mary's plan.

A few weeks before Richard's death, Mary had gone to the shop run by Edward Thomas, another of the druggists in the new town, with a scrap of paper on which was written 'one pennyworth of arsenic for destroying rats', claiming that there were rats in the kitchen. Mr Thomas carefully warned her of the dangers of the poison and labelled it to that effect also. She returned again for more arsenic on Saturday, 2 November, saying there was still one rat in the kitchen. Mary had also purchased another poison, *nux vomica* (strychnine), from yet another druggist, William Abrahams, on the pretext of poisoning mice.

When her father got home from the works on the Saturday afternoon he said he'd have some arrowroot. Mary gave him the powder for it and he mixed it with milk and sugar himself. After an hour or so he complained the concoction had an odd taste and sent Mary back to the shop where she had bought the arrowroot. Mrs Pickersgill tasted it, found no fault and Mary insisted on taking it away with her. Arsenic was kept at the shop, stored very carefully, and Mr Pickersgill used it to kill mice in his own house, mixed with lard and oatmeal, and had possibly sold some to Mr Gallop on occasions for use in the medications he'd made for men in the works. Arsenic was widely used as a treatment for a vast range of disorders, including skin diseases, arthritis and angina.

Later on the Saturday evening Richard rapidly became severely ill, and the lodger William Frazer went to fetch a doctor, Mr George Stephenson. On examining the patient,

Dr Stephenson concluded that the patient was suffering from cholera as he was vomiting so much and his extremities were cold. He prescribed hot water and hot salt to try and warm his hands and feet. On the Friday and Saturday nights of that fatal weekend, Mary and her sister also suffered bouts of vomiting. Frazer the lodger had noticed that there was something odd about the arrowroot mixture that Gallop had left in the bowl; it had a yellow froth and a hot taste as if it contained cayenne pepper. But when he returned a little later with the doctor, it had been poured away and the bowl washed. Richard was vomiting and in pain all night and died at 7.30 am on the Sunday morning.

Mary's immediate reaction was to ask the lodger to get her a free railway pass to go Liverpool, which he refused to do. She then assisted in the laying-out of the body. By 11 am Assistant Constable Michael Kenty had arrived, obviously with some suspicions. He took a statement, and at this point Mary was allowed to get a handkerchief from a drawer. As she did so, Constable Kenty took it from her and saw she was also clutching a packet labelled '*nux vomica* poison', bought she explained for killing rats. He searched the house and confiscated bread, cheese, flour and cakes for testing. Mary, meanwhile, in the process of folding clothes and putting them away in a chest of drawers tried to hide a packet. The constable spotted this, and was very clear that he had already searched that particular drawer and it had not been there before. The packet contained a white powder. It would appear that the constable's suspicions were confirmed and he took Mary into custody.

Tests carried out at the Liverpool Apothecaries Hall showed the packet to be equal measures of arrowroot and arsenic. The food taken from the house, including flour, also showed traces of arsenic. This explained the attack of vomiting that the sisters had suffered. Mary had made cakes and bread on Friday for the family and it would appear had been careless with the poison, or the cakes had somehow got mixed up, as she had put arsenic in one of them that was meant for her father, but he didn't eat it. A post-mortem examination of the body by Mr Stephenson found inflammation from the gullet to the rectum, signs that were characteristic of arsenical poisoning, and there was also some of the substance still in the stomach. He noted, incidentally, that people in Crewe were in the habit of doctoring themselves, presumably suspecting that the deceased had been careless when self-administering the substance for his bowel complaint.

Mary, said to be rather a short girl with a florid complexion, pleaded not guilty at her trial. Her defence counsel argued that Richard Gallop had been self-medicating with arsenic for several weeks, which conceivably he could have done, as he was interested in medications and indeed prescribed them to others.

Some of the houses originally built for the new railway workers at Crewe. (Susan Chambers)

He had not wanted his family to call in the doctor, pointed out the counsel, and he had mixed his arrowroot and milk himself, and the poison he had been using for medicinal purposes had got into the flour by mistake, he suggested. He conceded that Mary might well have inherited her mother's insanity, but thought it most unlikely that a 'trivial quarrel' with her father over the young man would have pushed her to such an act as murder.

In summing up, the judge displayed little patience with the insanity argument. The question was, he said, had she deliberately administered poison? The jury deliberated for what the press called 'a considerable time' and decided she was guilty, but recommended her to mercy. To this the judge asked rhetorically 'On what grounds can you recommend the prisoner to mercy for the murder of her own father?' and sentenced her to hang. Mary then, as throughout the case, showed no emotion. On her return to gaol she made a statement in the presence of a magistrate and the chaplain of Chester Castle, being a full confession of her guilt, and included the sentence: 'If I could have opened my mind to anybody, and had received a little good advice, I am sure I would not have committed the crime.'

The Revd Dr Penny, the magistrate who witnessed that statement, organised a petition requesting the exercise of the Royal prerogative of mercy and commutation of the sentence to transportation on several grounds. This made reference to the fact that her life up to this point had probably been irreproachable and she had been teacher in a Wesleyan Methodist school. The crime, it was suggested, was not long premeditated and she had no great hatred of her father, but was distressed at not being able to marry the person she wanted. She could spend a useful penitential life teaching in the place to where she might be transported, the Chester public would be spared the revolting spectacle of a young female being executed and the jury had in fact recommended mercy. Although her possible insanity was not mentioned in the petition, great emphasis was placed on this by the press. The petition was signed by the Bishop of Chester and the Chancellor of the diocese, who were criticised by certain wings of the press for a desire to palliate parricide or weaken the objections of the moral law. Two Nantwich Methodist ministers refused to sign it in addition to the Revd John Cooper, the rector of Coppenhall, who a couple of years earlier had been responsible for pointing out to the founders of the new railway community that they should have a church to cater for spiritual needs. There was also a petition organised by the Revd Taylor, rector of St Peter's, Chester, signed by women of that town, and one from the people of Crewe and Nantwich. John Tollemache, the South Cheshire Tory MP, helped to present the petitions to the Home Secretary. But the widespread support for mercy proved to be in vain when the Secretary of State announced he could see no justification for recommending Her Majesty to show clemency. This disappointing news was only received at a late hour on the day before the date set for the hanging. As executions were carried out at the Chester City Gaol, Mary was moved there from the Castle in the early hours of the morning to avoid the attentions of the crowds. Her last few days in the County Gaol had been spent almost entirely on religious matters with the care of the chaplain of the gaol and Mr Rowe, a Primitive Methodist minister from Chester. The matron, Mrs Bennion, was said to be as good to her as a mother would have been.

A dreadful irony, which must have been as difficult for Mary to bear as almost anything else, was the fact that the object of her affection, when asked by Mary's sister on her behalf to go and see her before she died, had refused, and expressed his thankfulness that he was in no way implicated in the murder.

Chapter 8

The Violent Death of PC Green

Once a year Cheshire Police hold a memorial day to remember officers who have fallen in the line of duty. Top of this list, chronologically speaking, is Police Constable James Green, of Elworth, whose body was dragged from the Trent and Mersey Canal on Friday, 28 February 1873. Nobody was ever convicted of causing his death, though a neighbour was arrested and tried.

This story begins at the November Sessions in 1872, when James Buckley was found guilty of stealing straw from the farm of Kester Kettell of Moston. (Students of Crewe's history might be interested to learn that Kester Kettell was grandfather to the mayor of Crewe in 1916.) The principal witness to the crime was PC James Green who, after hiding himself in an outhouse, saw Buckley carrying a sheaf from the direction of Kettell's farm. His defence was that he had been given the straw, but, as Kettell denied this, Buckley was found guilty and had to serve one month's hard labour. The *Crewe Guardian* claimed that Green was the type of policeman that struck terror into the hearts of the lower classes.

On Monday, 24 February 1875, James Green informed Inspector Hulme that, being certain Buckley was up to his old tricks, he would watch his premises all night to catch him red-handed. He refused the offer of another officer to keep him company on this lonely vigil. According to his wife, who never saw him alive again, he left home at around 7 pm, after eating a hearty meal. A strange element in this case, that says much about the lax control in the police service of those days, is that his absence was not noted until his wife reported him missing on Wednesday. The next day (Thursday), Inspector Hulme instructed PC Thomas Jones, stationed at Wheelock, to search the ditches and fields near to Buckley's house, at Elton Moss, so it would seem that Buckley was already a strong suspect, even before the body was found.

On the Friday the search was taken up again, this time with Superintendent Rowbottom and PCs Williamson and Booth, specifically to drag the Trent and Mersey Canal. All the equipment needed for this had to borrowed from locals, as the police did not seem to possess their own. On receipt of private information, Inspector Hulme went to Buckley's home to question him about scratches on his face, bruises around his eyes and cuts on his hands. His explanation was that the injuries had been received when he fell out of a neighbour's apple tree that he was pruning. They were also interested in the clothes he had been wearing and whether he had seen Green that week.

While they were with Buckley, the awful news was received that Green's body had been found. John Booth, who had been dragging the canal, discovered the submerged corpse near to Moss Bridge, the nearest section of canal to Buckley's cottage. The mutilated remains of the 36-year-old policemen were wheeled on a cart to Arthur Pointon's barn, which is where Inspector Hulme brought the suspect, James Buckley. The *Crewe Chronicle* report made it plain that Buckley seemed unaware then that he was on the police list of suspects for the murder of PC Green. After viewing the body, Hulme arrested him on suspicion of causing the death of the constable, an accusation that caused Buckley great agitation.

Returning to the prisoner's house, the police now began a thorough search, removing various blood-stained items that interested them, such as a striped waistcoat, pieces of sacking, a freshly washed shirt, an axe, spade, wheelbarrow and a portion of the house yard. Also examined was the apple tree that Buckley claimed he had slipped from while odd-jobbing for his neighbour, Mr Hill. On the Saturday, the police returned to the cottage again, and in addition interviewed Martha Buckley, the prisoner's wife and the mother of their 16-month-old son. She also had two other sons, from a previous marriage, living in the matrimonial home. On the evidence of little more than the freshly washed shirt, Martha was arrested as an accomplice to the murder of PC Green.

Buckley was described as tall and cadaverous looking with very black hair when he appeared before J St John Yates, magistrate at Sandbach, on Saturday, 1 March. As might be expected, the courtroom was crowded with onlookers very unsympathetic to Buckley, who had to be guarded at all times for his own safety. Dr Charles Latham, having completed a post-mortem examination early that morning, described the injuries. He had counted twenty-three cuts around the head and face, none of which would have caused the policeman's death. This was mainly due to the rupturing of the bladder, with shock from the cuts as a contributory factor. His opinion was that the injury to the bladder was caused by a heavy kick. An examination of the stomach and bowel led him to believe that about 8 hours had passed since the constable had last eaten. He also remarked that Green had been remarkably healthy and a fine specimen of a man. After a rambling statement from the son of a neighbour, the magistrate remanded Buckley in the local lock-up. Later that day his wife joined him, but not in the same cell.

Elworth church was crowded for Constable Green's funeral, which was conducted with due solemnity by the Revd G Littlewood. Some estimates suggest that 2,000 onlookers watched the procession led by 4 constables, with the coffin on their shoulders. Along with his 26-year-old wife Mary, their 5-year-old son (a younger son did not seem to be present) and other relatives, Superintendent Rowbottom, Inspector Hulme and twenty constables in full uniform also attended. The awful

The gravestone of PC James Green in St Peter's Church, Elworth.
(Peter Ollerhead)

outrage of the murder of a policeman had not occurred in the Cheshire force before. Large crowds also visited Buckley's cottage for the macabre purpose of gleaning mementos from what they imagined was a murder scene.

When the remanded man and his wife appeared before the coroner, W R Dunstan, at the resumed inquest they were represented by a barrister from Hanley, named Richardson. With very carefully worded questions he elicited such facts that Buckley's facial injuries resulted from sliding and bumping from the tree in Mr Hill's garden, rather than a straight fall. Hulme also had to admit that he had not discovered any signs of a struggle on Buckley's premises. Richardson's request for a discharge for Martha Buckley was refused, despite Dr Dixon, of Northwich, giving her a glowing character reference.

After a further adjournment, the inquest continued later in the week, when still further challenges were made to the police case against Buckley and his wife. Campbell Brown, of the Liverpool Royal Infirmary School of Medicine, after examining the items given to him by the police, testified that they were bloodstained, but whether animal or human he could not say. Richardson also established that the police had not bothered to investigate Buckley's claim that most of the blood on his clothes was from killing a pig. As the evidence against Martha Buckley was negligible, she was discharged after nine days inside, much to the relief of her parents and husband. It was decided that a case had been made against Buckley sufficient to progress his case to the assizes.

Buckley's trial there took place early in April 1873, under the jurisdiction of Mr Justice Lush. Strangely, one of the prosecuting team had unsuccessfully defended the prisoner at his theft trial the previous year. Buckley had been the first and only suspect for the murder, even before a body was discovered, a fact that seems to have flawed the police inquiries. There were five or six reasons given for Buckley being in the dock, the major one being the grudge he had against Green for testifying against him at his trial for stealing hay. Prosecution witnesses testified that he had uttered threats against him for fabricating evidence. Scratches and injuries on his face were caused, according to the police, by a struggle with Green, not a fall or slide from an apple tree. Bloodstains on the prisoner's clothes were from the many cuts on the policeman's head and face. Buckley's house was near to the canal, where the body was found. Late on in the investigations another factor had been added, when the police suggested that a knife, found in Buckley's cottage, belonged to the murdered policeman.

Dr Latham repeated the evidence he had given previously in

his post-mortem examination report. Inspector Joseph Hulme spoke in moving terms of the intelligence and reliability of Green as a constable: 'in whom I had more confidence than others, and he had more latitude than others.' This latter point is important, as the police were criticised for not instituting the search earlier than they did. Apparently, Green had the freedom to pursue investigations on his own account, even to the point of carrying a privately owned pistol when he went out that Monday night. Despite objections from the defence team, Hulme was allowed to give verbal evidence of a conversation he had on the 24th (outlined above), when Green told him that he was convinced that Buckley was 'up to his old tricks'.

Later in the trial, George Lewis, a farmer of Moston, witnessed that he had seen Green at Tattnall's public house (Railway Hotel) on the 24th dressed in a corded jacket and an old hat. He went on to say that the oddly dressed policeman went towards Burgesses (Fox Inn). This was confirmed by Joseph Wakefield, a plate layer of Bradwall, who also saw Green coming out of Tattnall's that evening. Further testimony elucidated that Green did not leave Tattnall's until at least 8 pm, after drinking a glass of ale. Another witness claimed he saw him in his disguise on Moston Bridge on the Monday evening.

Even the coroner at the inquest picked up on these movements of Green that seemed shrouded in ambiguity: 'The more light thrown on the movements of the deceased the greater the mystery appeared to rise.' The defence made much of this by pointing out that Green had refused the offer of help, because to send another officer, at 9 pm, would be too late as he would be in hiding near to Buckley's cottage long before then.

Various members of the Phillips family, whose cottage shared the same roof as the prisoner's, testified that Buckley was at home at 9 pm. They also said that there were no strange noises indicating a fight or a scuffle during the night, or anything unusual about the premises when they rose in the morning, when the yard was covered with a light scattering of snow.

Mrs Phillips also confirmed that James Buckley had killed a pig about three weeks before. It was high on the police agenda to prove that the blood on Buckley's clothes did not come from the pig.

A further area of dispute concerned blood on another waistcoat and on some cobbles in the yard that Buckley agreed had not come from the pig, maintaining rather that, while his wife was at her job in Crewe, his young son had cut himself with a knife. Dr Latham, after examining the child's hand, was doubtful the faint marks he could see would have bled very profusely. This positive testimony for the prosecution was damaged by the defence proving that the investigating team had not bothered to examine the child's pinafore when asked, which Buckley claimed bore unmistakeable signs of much bleeding. It has to be said that the suggestion by the police that scratches on flagstones in Buckley's yard had been caused by Green's boots is stretching credulity. Even the learned judge dismissed this with the remark that they could have been caused by anyone.

Thomas Alcock, a watchmaker of Sandbach, who had examined the policeman's watch, noted that it had stopped at 3.19, approximately 7 hours into its cycle, the glass was broken and the fingers damaged. He was of the opinion that this had been caused when the instrument came heavily into contact with cinder, or similar material, used for making paths. Obviously, the watch was full of water.

A resident of Elton Moss, Joseph Turner, who lived about 160yd from Moss Bridge, had heard 'unpleasant voices' on Monday or Tuesday night. Boats often tied up near to the bridge waiting for first light before moving on. As has already been noted, the body of Green was found some 50yd from the bridge.

Another area of dispute between the defence and the prosecution was whether the wounds to Green could have been caused by a boat after his body entered the water. Some witnesses, such as Dr Latham, were convinced the cuts to the head and face were administered before death, whereas John

The Trent and Mersey Canal at Moss Bridge, Moston, where the body of PC Green was found. (Peter Ollerhead)

Hill, who had worked for the canal company for over half a century, said that he had lifted many bodies out of the canal, some mutilated by the boats while others were untouched. Apparently, the undersides of the boats were plated with iron which, when it worked loose, could do severe damage to bodies in the canal. Other witnesses denied this was possible in Green's case. Defence counsel made much of the confusion and conflicting testimony regarding the injuries to the face and head, underlining to the jury that the doctor's evidence was at variance with other witnesses for the prosecution.

When the prosecuting team had finished, Mr Bowen rose to begin a speech to the jury that lasted 80 minutes, reviewing the police case against Buckley. Charles Latham had testified that Green was not struck from behind, a point that agreed with the police suggestion that Buckley received the scratches and black eye in his fight with Green. Was it likely, Mr Bowen proposed, that in a straight fight Buckley would have overwhelmed a younger, fitter man, with a pistol and a police whistle in his pocket. If they had had a fight, where did it take place, as testimony had been received that no noises or scuffles were reported at Buckley's cottage.

If Green had been killed on the 24th, where had his body been hidden, and how was Buckley supposed to have got it into the canal without being observed? Another fact, linked to the 24th, was the lack of food in the stomach and bowel when the corpse was examined. To the defence's mind, the blood on the various garments and items had been sufficiently explained as coming from the pig killing and the cut hand of Buckley's young son.

Buckley had cooperated with the police, pointing out the locations of all the various items that he had worn the previous week. Was this the action of a guilty man? Surely, a guilty man would have got rid of anything that would have incriminated him? The knife that various constables swore belonged to Green was a common item that could be purchased from many shops. Why would a murderer, whose motive was revenge, steal a cheap item that was easily found at Buckley's residence? Vengeance was a motive that could be applied to others convicted by Green's detecting skill.

The discrepancy between where the deceased constable said he would be and where he was actually seen on the 24th was raised, in addition to the conflicting statements regarding the child's pinafore. The police denied that Buckley had asked for it to be examined, whereas Dr Latham and another policeman testified that they had heard Buckley request that it be checked for blood stains.

When Mr Bowen concluded his long speech, the judge summed up and directed the jury to consider their verdict. This they did for 10 minutes before returning to pronounce James Buckley not guilty of the murder of Police Constable James Green. Large numbers of people waited outside the court room to catch a glimpse of the freed prisoner. Further crowds gathered at Crewe for the Chester train to arrive, so that they too might gain a moment of fame by describing the sight of a man recently on trial for his life.

When all is told, this neutral writer agrees with the judgement of the editor of the *Crewe Chronicle*, who wrote, in the issue after the trial, that he supported the jury's verdict. From a careful reading of accounts of the court proceedings, reported in different newspapers, it has to be said that the police did not muster a very satisfactory case against Buckley.

Green's death left a young widow, who herself was extremely ill, with three young children and no means of support. Subscription lists were opened to provide sufficient funds for Mary Green's sustenance. The county police committee awarded her a year's wages, £66 18s 4d, from the superannuation fund, while the magistrates circularised the various benches for help. Just over £34 was collected by the Lancashire force, and another £52 from Green's colleagues in Cheshire. Crewe magistrates, led by Wilmot Eardley, amassed £60 16s 9d. Individuals, such as Lord Egerton, of Tatton, subscribed generously, though it was all to no avail for Mrs Green as she sadly she lost her struggle with illness. Just fourteen weeks after James Green's burial, the grave was opened to admit her coffin, after being carried there, at her wish, by four uniformed constables. All the subscribed money was to be administered for her children's benefit by two trustees.

James Buckley returned to his life as a gardener and farm labourer, near to the canal at Moston. According to the 1881 census, he described himself as a widower, living on the Moss with his son, Arthur. He died so suddenly, in September 1896, that the coroner had to be informed. His inquiries established that Buckley's death, at 69, was from natural causes.

Now all the dust has settled, it is indisputable that when James Green was murdered Cheshire police lost a brave and intelligent officer. The resulting botched investigation let him down, along with his wife, son and colleagues, though, as we have seen, his wife only lived another fourteen weeks. Some person, or persons unknown, was responsible for the death of a family man, whose paid task (at just over £1 a week) was to uphold the law. So many years have now passed that we shall never know the identity of these desperadoes. All we can do is to salute the memory and example of PC James Green.

Chapter 9

Two Murders in Two Weeks

The death of an infant

Crewe had not been riven by rumours of murder since Mary Gallop poisoned her father in 1844, but this changed in May 1875. A distressed James Halfpenny hurried to Hightown to inform his father-in-law, George Rhead, that Thomas Halfpenny, his infant son, had been killed. As this is a sad case involving insanity, only the outline will be considered and that because it is the first of two murders separated by only a couple of weeks.

When the inquest into the infant's death was held, in the Commercial Hotel, the bereaved father reported the salient details of how he found his 2-week-old son covered with blood in his cot on Saturday, 22 May. He had gone upstairs to change his clothes, leaving his wife ironing a shirt in the kitchen with his son and his brother-in-law, Charles. She then left Charles alone with the child, while she took her husband a freshly ironed shirt, before placing the other laundered items in a chest of drawers in the bedroom.

When James Halfpenny descended to the kitchen, he noticed blood on a pocket knife in his brother-in-law's hand. As both he and his wife had been concerned over the strange behaviour of Charles, he immediately thought he had deliberately injured himself. To his horror, he heard him exclaim that he had hurt the baby, and on examination found that his infant son was bleeding from several wounds. When Dr Richard Lord answered the urgent summons to the Halfpenny's home he had to silence a crowd of shrieking women, from neighbouring dwellings, before he sadly pronounced the infant dead.

At the trial at Chester Assizes, evidence was given by Dr Richard Lord and Dr Thomas Bailey that the prisoner, Halfpenny's brother-in-law, was unfit to understand the charge, as he was of an unsound mind. Testimony was also given that in addition to complaining of pains in his head, he had also been very despondent for about two months. It was reported that a retired Wesleyan Methodist minister, after praying with him, had said that unless they kept a sharp eye on Charlie somebody would be hurt. Sadly, as 'they' did not follow the advice, a baby boy was killed.

James Halfpenny testified that the prisoner, who had lodged with them for about three years, was of a sober disposition, and always considerate to his sister and her children. Charles had always shown love and care for all the children, especially the newborn child on whom he seemed to dote. Halfpenny added that neither he, nor his wife, ever imagined that the infant's uncle was capable of such a dreadful deed. There was very little other evidence needed, as it was obvious who had held the knife. All that had to be considered was the prisoner's state of mind at the time. After the jury returned its verdict, the unfortunate man was sentenced, by Lord Chief Justice Cockburn, to be detained in strict custody, at Her Majesty's pleasure, in Broadmoor Hospital, which had opened about ten years earlier.

A few weeks after the trial, a notice appeared in the *Crewe Chronicle* from the friends and relatives of the imprisoned man, thanking the public for the generous assistance that had enabled them to procure counsel and legal representation for the trial, at Chester. Twelve years later, in 1887, the local paper reported that, though he was much better mentally, Charles was still detained in the Sandhurst Asylum (Broadmoor), where he had been made bandmaster of the hospital's small brass band.

Sometime in the next few years he was well enough to be released into the community. By 1901 he was back in Crewe, lodging once more in the West Street home of the forgiving and gracious James and Mary Halfpenny, along with his mother, Martha Rhead.

Infamy in Station Street

Just two days after the inquest into the Halfpenny murder, George Henry Goosey, a 31-year-old unemployed bricklayer, called at the police station in Crewe. At 10 minutes past 9 on 1 June 1875 he reported the sudden death of Jane Mountfield, a 77-year-old widow. At first her death seemed to be the result of a straightforward accident, yet as the police investigated, it was soon apparent that it was more a case of straightforward murder.

Looking east along Station Street, c. 1967. The last building on the north side of the street is the Queen's Hotel, previously the North Western Hotel.
(Peter Ollerhead)

Goosey had married Jane Mountfield's daughter, also named Jane, and lived with her and their three children in his mother-in-law's house in Station Street, and had done so for about ten years. He was often unemployed, owing to his intemperate habits, coupled with a vicious temper. His laziness meant that the home was straitened, with little to eat, and oftentimes the old lady was fed by the lodger, or neighbours, as she was not ashamed to beg when hunger overcame her pride.

Station Street, on the east side of Mill Street, comprised small terraced houses, containing a couple of ground-floor rooms, a tiny kitchen and two or three bedrooms. These properties had been erected to service the needs of the motive power sheds, at the eastern end of the street. In such cramped conditions it was impossible for neighbours to be unaware of deteriorating relationships in any of the nearby dwellings.

Goosey's home was not a happy one, owing mainly to his offensive attitude and propensity for beer, which was easily available as there were at least sixteen pubs within 300yd of his home. Occasionally, he worked as a distraint bailiff, once having recourse to the courts when he was assaulted by an irate iron moulder, whose house he was emptying. Most of Goosey's aggressiveness was directed at his mother-in-law, but as they lived in her house he could hardly evict her. Consequently, he had many times been heard to say that he wished her dead, even throwing heavy objects at her when his moodiness was particularly intense. Usually, his wife was able to intervene between him and her mother, ameliorating his tantrums by bearing the brunt of his anger on her own body. Even Jane Palmer, the lodger, kept a poker close by in case she was attacked when Goosey's violence was at its height. She later testified, at Goosey's trial, that she had heard him tell his children to kick the 'old b—' if she tried to correct them.

On this particular summer's day, George Goosey came home to Station Street at about 4.45 pm. His wife went into the small backyard to chop firewood, leaving Goosey in the kitchen, along with the elderly Jane Mountfield and his three children. Jane Palmer was preparing a meal for her husband Henry, a labourer with the London & North Western Railway Company. This scene provides an incidental insight into the communal arrangements of many households in Victorian Crewe, where a family's income could be supplemented by subletting a room, despite the house being overcrowded to start with.

At about 5pm, the old lady went to the front door of her house to watch a funeral procession, as the hearse, pulled by a horse, slowly made its solemn way along Station Street and into Mill Street. After chatting with a passer-by for a few minutes, she returned to the back-kitchen, where Goosey was waiting for his wife to make him a meal. Before long, Jane Palmer could hear angry words being exchanged between him and Jane Mountfield. A contributory factor to the bad relationship was that the elder Jane was quite deaf, which meant she did not always realise that somebody was talking to her, or hear the noise that she herself was creating.

On this occasion Jane had dropped something, generating a string of oaths and curses from Goosey. This led to an exchange of loud comments during which Mrs Mountfield was heard to say, 'Don't curse me. Every time you come in you start to curse me', to which Goosey replied, 'I'll give you a smash in the mouth.' The next thing was the sound of a heavy thud, as the old lady fell to the floor, and on investigation Jane Palmer found her lying full length, with her head towards the door. Two of the children were crying, causing Goosey to threaten them with more violence. Jane Palmer later claimed that she heard the eldest boy blame his father for knocking his grandma down with a stick.

In response to all of this commotion, Jane Goosey hurried in from her chopping labours in the yard to join Jane Palmer in her efforts to revive the unconscious septuagenarian, and to staunch the bleeding from a wound above the right ear. Neither George Goosey nor his wife seemed inclined to send for a doctor, stating that she would soon come round. Eventually, when Jane had recovered sufficiently to be propped upon a chair, she was given the usual working class remedy of a sip of brandy. As the patient was drifting in and out of consciousness, Jane Goosey and Jane Palmer carried her up to her bed. George Goosey still refused to allow a doctor to be called, as he claimed that 'the old devil is only foxing'. This was at approximately 6.15 pm, about an hour after she fallen.

Some 15 minutes later Jane Mountfield, now deeply unconscious, began fitting, yet still no one went for medical assistance, as Goosey confidently asserted that bathing her face with vinegar would work a cure. He was now stating that Mrs Mountfield had banged her head against a cupboard when she fell. Sometime around 7.00 pm, Jane Palmer, who was showing far more concern for the old lady than George Goosey, noticed a change in Mrs Mountfield's breathing, and urged Jane Goosey to send for a doctor immediately, or face much trouble if she died.

Despite his misgivings, George Goosey, who was at the Engine Tavern in Mill Street, finally relented, and walked from the public house to call on Dr Thomas Bailey at his surgery, in Havelock House. When his evening surgery was over, Dr Bailey called to see Mrs Mountfield, instructing Jane Palmer to follow him back to the surgery for some medicine. Before she could return, the old lady breathed her last, succumbing to the injuries she had sustained some 3^1/$_2$ hours earlier.

Following his visit to the police station to report this sudden death, Goosey began to exhibit signs of disquiet. To some neighbours he said that he had only given his mother-in-law a gentle push, to others he suggested that she had taken a giddy turn. At 15 minutes to midnight on 1 June the police had sufficient evidence to arrest George Goosey for murdering Jane Mountfield. When he attempted to escape, through his back door, he found PC William Wynne there ready to escort him to the cells, to await a magistrates' hearing, despite his protestations that he was innocent.

While Goosey was on remand, an inquest into Jane Mountfield's death was held at the Commercial Hotel, on the corner of High Street, under the jurisdiction of the coroner Dunstan. Dr Thomas Bailey reported that death resulted from bleeding in the brain, caused by a fracture of the skull. Other witnesses testified to the bad feelings that existed between George Goosey and his mother-in-law. Jane Palmer claimed that Jane Goosey had hinted that she should amend her evidence to portray George Goosey in a better light, because the living were more important than the dead. It all made little difference, as the inquest jury returned a verdict of manslaughter.

At a reconvened magistrates' hearing, before W Tollemache and Major Starkie on 12 June, further evidence that had been unearthed by the police resulted in them charging Goosey with wilfully murdering his mother-in-law, with malice aforethought. Jane Palmer's husband, Henry, testified that he had heard Goosey threaten to kick his wife's ribs if she continued to contradict him. Sarah Foley, who had lived next door to the Gooseys for eight years, swore that she had regularly seen bruises on Jane Mountfield's arms, caused by her son-in-law's violence. Another neighbour asserted that Goosey had told her that the old lady fell while she was placing a heavy pan on the fire, an excuse that he used on the coroner's form, when he reported the old lady's death. The police proved that there was no fire in the grate and that there was no coal on the premises.

Dr Bailey, when called as a witness, suggested that the house poker had been used to cause the skull fracture, as the indentation on the old lady's head exactly fitted the shape of the poker. He also stated that, in his opinion, the injuries could not have been caused by a fall against a cupboard. During this time Goosey, according to the reporter from the *Crewe Chronicle*, showed extreme nervousness by consistently biting his nails and twitching his forehead. After conferring for a few minutes, the magistrates committed him to be tried for the murder of Jane Mountfield at the Chester Summer Assizes.

Lord Chief Justice Cockburn, who a couple of days before had sentenced another Crewe man to be detained at Her Majesty's pleasure for the murder of his nephew, presided over Goosey's trial, with Mr Burke Wood leading for the Crown, and the Honourable Charles Swettenham for the defence. It is pertinent and germane that the low esteem and lack of regard for Goosey, especially in the Mill Street area and the town of Crewe generally, meant that a defence fund was not organised by friends and neighbours.

The police maintained that Goosey had hit his mother-in-law with a blunt instrument, as the wound was caused, according to Dr Bailey, by a downward blow from the poker. Swettenham posed the only possible defence argument that Goosey was

One of the many pubs near to Goosey's home, 1960s. (Peter Ollerhead)

guilty of manslaughter, rather than murder. Mounfield's death was caused by a fall and not a blow, he claimed, as the poker was found in its usual place free from blood stains. He made much of the cramped conditions in which the family lived, and that this led inevitably to family strife. For Goosey to be guilty of murdering the old lady he had to have been motivated by an intention to kill, or cause grievous bodily harm. Swettenham claimed the word 'intend' was pregnant with importance, stating that Goosey, in addition to cursing his wife and children, was sometimes violent with them, yet never desired their deaths.

In his summing up after a 9-hour trial, the Lord Chief Justice charged the jury to decide carefully between manslaughter and murder, as Goosey was obviously guilty of causing the death of Jane Mountfield. After retiring for less than 10 minutes, the jury returned with a verdict of manslaughter, much to the relief of the prisoner. Before he sentenced him to life imprisonment, the judge remarked that the jury had taken a merciful view, with which he tended to agree. He also said that blood was upon the hands of Goosey and: 'it is my duty to mark my sense of the brutal inhumanity of your conduct by visiting you with the heaviest judgement and sentence that can be pronounced by law. The sentence that I pass on you is that you be kept in penal servitude for the rest of your life.' And so it was that George Henry Goosey disappeared from the town of Crewe, where he had behaved in a violent and dissolute way for over twelve years. It was Jane Mountfield's misfortune that her daughter conceived a child by this brute of a man and then, according to the conventions of the day, had to marry him. It was a greater catastrophe for the mother-in-law that Goosey could not provide a home for his pregnant wife. Sadly, Jane Goosey was not capable of keeping the home together, as the three young daughters of the couple are recorded, in 1881, as living in the Nantwich Union Workhouse.

In the national census of 1891, George Goosey is registered as a convict on the returns from the gaol in Lydford, Devon, or, as it is usually known, Dartmoor Prison. By the time of the 1901 census he had been released on parole, after serving around eighteen years. By this time he was living with an Isabella Goosey, though whether he was ever divorced from his previous wife is not known. After leaving prison he did not return to Crewe, preferring to live in Northamptonshire, the county of his birth. Aged 57 years old at this time and, according to the census return, still laying bricks, one hopes that while in prison he had learned to curb his temper or, if not, that Isabella's mother did not live with them.

Chapter 10

The Brutal Slaying of Aunt Sarah

In 1887, Saturday morning was part of the working week for employees at the LNWR works in Crewe, unless they were on short time, which was the case for some foundry workers in March of that year. Amongst these was Thomas Henry Bevan, an apprentice iron moulder, whose life would not have ended as it did if he had been at work on 27 March. Many of Crewe's working men had arranged to travel that day to Middlewich, where Crewe Alexandra were playing Davenham in the final of the Cheshire Football Association Challenge Cup. Again, if Thomas Henry Bevan had decided to make that trip to support the Alex, his life would have moved along different lines.

Instead of working, or anticipating the match, Bevan had a late breakfast and then left his lodgings at the east end of West Street. He walked along Albert Street and Meredith Street into Market Street, crossed the Leighton Brook into Henry Street and paid a visit to his Aunt Sarah in the neighbouring township of Church Coppenhall. She was one of four Welsh sisters who, with their husbands, had migrated to the town in search of work in the LNWR railway works. One of these sisters, Hannah, Bevan's mother, had died some years earlier causing him to seek lodgings with relatives. In 1887, he was living in Orchard Place, off West Street, with his Aunt Ellen and Uncle Thomas Clutton, while making regular visits at weekends to Henry Street, where his mother's two other sisters lived.

When Bevan lived at the parental home in Warmingham he refused to attend school regularly. This resulted in him being sent by the local magistrates to a reformatory, or young offenders' institution, for about five years. He must have received a reasonable level of education there for him to be accepted as an apprentice in the LNWR iron foundry. Along with reading, writing and arithmetic he must also have received rudimentary tutoring in the art of theft. He was suspected of stealing his cousin's watch and a gold sovereign, much to the detriment of his relationship with his Uncle James Parsons, who worked in the same iron foundry. In addition to this, he took a watch from the Clutton home, which he returned to the owner the same day, perhaps because his conscience was pricked. Owing to these tendencies, Bevan was always being told by his Aunt Sarah to be a good boy.

Another uncle, Henry Griffiths, aged 63, was not on short time and was at his labouring job that Saturday morning from 6.30 am until he finished at noon. He stopped at Ellen and Thomas Clutton's house in Orchard Place for a few minutes before he made his way home. Henry and his 59-year-old wife Sarah, a small, rather overweight lady who had not been well for a few days, lived in Church Coppenhall. At that date Church Coppenhall was not part of the town of Crewe or Monks Coppenhall, being on the northern side of the Leighton Brook, which formed the boundary between the townships. Also living with them was an adopted 10-year-old niece, Mary Jones, who, it was rumoured, had replaced Thomas Bevan in the list of beneficiaries in the Griffiths' will. Apparently, the original had been revoked in favour of the girl because of Bevan's record of petty thieving.

Henry and Sarah Griffiths dwelt in a recently built terraced house in the unmade Henry Street, hard against the Primitive Methodist chapel, which had been erected seven years earlier in 1880. Another of the four Welsh sisters, Elizabeth Parsons, lived with her family in an adjoining cottage. Both Sarah and

Henry Street Primitive Methodist chapel, opened in 1880. (Bernard Owen)

Elizabeth regularly attended the evening service at this small and unfashionable newly built chapel.

On entering his home, at around 12.30 pm, Griffiths noticed a broken dolly-peg lying on the floor. (A dolly-peg was a stout wooden instrument around a metre long that was used on washday.) On moving into the front kitchen he was met by the dreadful spectacle of his wife lying prone upon the floor, covered with blood, along with the recumbent figure of Mary

Jones. Initially, Griffiths thought his wife had suffered a fit and went next door seeking the help of his sister-in-law, Elizabeth Parsons. After examining her sister, Elizabeth realised the serious nature of her injuries and swiftly sent Griffiths to Hightown to fetch Dr Moody.

Meanwhile, Willie Parsons, Bevan's cousin, went to Orchard Place to inform the Cluttons (and Thomas Bevan), who all arrived to find that Dr Moody had concluded that Sarah Griffiths had died as a result of a violent attack. With open wounds to the back of the skull, along with indentations to the same region, and several broken ribs, he could hardly think otherwise. Next to the body was a damaged pair of bloodstained metal coal tongs that had obviously been used as a weapon upon one of the victims. James Parsons, Elizabeth's husband, dispatched Thomas Bevan to the police headquarters in Edleston Road to inform them of the incident. On returning to Henry Street, Bevan was asked to help carry his aunt's body upstairs before he returned to Orchard Place.

When Superintendent Leah arrived at Henry Street, at around 2.30 pm, inquiries commenced on the basis that tramps (a usual target for police interest), passing through the town, were guilty of the ferocious attack. Apparently, a number had been seen that morning selling from door to door in the immediate environs of Henry Street. As the murdered woman's purse was missing, along with the little girl's moneybox, robbery was the obvious motive, meaning many itinerants were interviewed over Saturday and Sunday. One man, an innocent seller of pins, was hauled out of his lodging house bed in Stafford Street to assist with inquiries. In addition, two jobless beggars were brought some 15 miles from Burslem in Staffordshire to be questioned on the strength of possible bloodstains on their clothes. Further arrests were also made in Sandbach and Northwich, where a begging tramp brought suspicion upon himself as he ran away down a narrow alley on seeing a policeman. Needless to say, the itinerant community did not take kindly to this rigorous police examination of their activities, all of which had been approved by the Chief Constable of Cheshire when he had visited the murder scene to be updated on the progress of the investigation.

In addition to suspected itinerant involvement, Superintendent Leah was following another, more promising, line of investigation, which concerned the nephew, Thomas Bevan. Instigated by a brief interview with the seriously injured niece, Mary Jones, he went personally to Orchard Place in search of Bevan. When she had regained consciousness for a short while, at around 4.00 pm, Mary managed to stammer that Tom Bevan was her assailant. At about half past four in the afternoon of Saturday, 26 March, he was arrested for further questioning into the murder of his aunt.

By Monday there was sufficient evidence to warrant a charge of murder being levied against Bevan before E R Bellyse, a county magistrate, and this meant that the tramp search was called off. Bevan was still on remand at Crewe when the mortal remains of Sarah Griffiths were buried in the graveyard of St Michael's, the mother church of the parish of Coppenhall. A deliberately extended route had been organised for the funeral procession from Henry Street, allowing the thousands of onlookers, who crowded the streets and burial ground, to witness the sad cortège on what was otherwise a fine, sunny day.

An inquest into the death was opened in the Cumberland Arms, under the jurisdiction of H C Yates, with Thomas Glover (owner of a grocer's shop at the corner of Earle Street and Market Street) as foreman. The chief witness, the child Mary Jones, was too ill to attend and only identification evidence was taken before the inquest was adjourned for a fortnight. This little girl had seven cuts to the left side of her face and forehead with another ten on the right, some penetrating to the bone. When the inquest was resumed, Dr J W Moody disclosed that Sarah Griffiths' death was caused by a concussion of the brain and loss of blood, consequent upon a broken rib bone penetrating the left lung. He opined that it would have taken her about 20 minutes to die, but she would have been rendered unconscious after the blows to the head. From this and other evidence, the bleak and dreadful story of how the callous murder had been committed began to unfold.

As was his custom when on short-time working, Bevan visited his aunt in Henry Street on a Saturday morning, usually arriving while they were having breakfast. On this particular day, Mary Jones went for the groceries and afterwards for some potatoes to the Co-operative Store in Market Street, about 300yd away. For this shopping trip and for paying John Fearn, the milkman, Sarah Griffiths needed money from her purse,

Orchard Place, where Thomas Bevan lodged in 1887. (Cheshire Archives and Local Studies)

which she kept in a chest, a fact that Bevan could not have failed to observe. It was proved by the distressed and bereaved Henry Griffiths that he had given his wages, of 18*s*, to his wife on Friday, 25 March, an amount that declined to almost 16*s* after she had paid for the groceries and milk.

While Mary Jones, who was Bevan's half-sister, was on her second visit to the Co-op Stores, Bevan felled Sarah Griffiths with a wooden dolly-peg. He then jumped on the unconscious woman many times, shattering her ribs. Before he could make his escape with the stolen purse, Mary entered through the back door carrying her bag of potatoes, and was attacked by him. She ran to the anticipated safety of her aunt in the front kitchen, only to be struck by Bevan again, with such ferocity that the pair of heavy coal tongs he used as a weapon was knocked out of shape. Leaving her dead, as he thought, he was seen leaving the cottage at around 11.40 am and walking towards Sheppard Street, across the waste ground that bounded a water filled marl pit, known locally as the 'razzer'. Other witnesses were found that testified that they had seen Bevan near to Henry Street or on his way through Crewe walking towards Orchard Place. Not one person could be located to support his alibi that he was walking around Crewe Hall Park all morning.

Though traces of blood were found on Bevan's clothes when they were examined by Dr Joseph Bell, the county analyst for Cheshire, what really placed Bevan in the frame was Mary Jones' deposition of the details of her attack in simple yet graphic detail:

> *I remember the day I was hurt. Tom Bevan hurt me. I remember him coming into the house. My aunt was in when he came. He sat down in the house. I went out to fetch the shop things and the potatoes. When I went out I left my aunt and Bevan in the house. When I came back with the potatoes I saw Thomas Bevan in the back kitchen. He took the*

potatoes off me and put them on the floor and then hurt me . . . he hurt my head. He kicked me. He hurt me very much in the head and back. I forget everything else after he got me onto the floor. I do not remember what he did besides. I did not see anything in his hands. Tom Bevan is the man who hurt me.

This was spoken in almost inaudible tones by the vulnerable young girl, with a heavily bandaged head, hardly able to stand unaided, having spent the weeks before the trial in Chester Royal Infirmary. The distressing sight of this dreadfully injured youngster, whispering her evidence at the Assize Court, before Mr Justice Denham, could not have helped the defence team, led by the Honourable R C Grosvenor, to persuade the jury of Bevan's innocence. Even when Grosvenor proved that some of her evidence was incorrect, it was excused as confusion of facts caused by the terrible beating she had received.

Before that happened, however, further evidence of Bevan's guilt was gleaned from a conversation he had with a fellow prisoner, who shared his cell at Knutsford, while Bevan was on remand. This man, Fred Gingell, who was serving six months for robbery, informed the prison authorities that Bevan had said he might plead guilty to assaulting Mary Jones, while denying murdering his aunt as no court would accept the evidence of Mary as she was under age. He also claimed that if found guilty he would maintain his innocence and only confess on the morning of his appointment with the scaffold, when he would shout: 'I did it, I'm guilty as I would not want to die with it on my conscience.' Further snatches of conversation included a discussion on the quality of food if one suffered the penalty of transportation, and most bizarre of all that if he was found guilty he was going to ask for good food at every meal. Regarding this last remark, Gingell advised him that his greatest need would be for a chaplain, and not food.

The trial at the end of July, delayed until that date by the inability of Mary Jones to appear, lasted for about 9 hours. Despite the best arguments of the defence team, the result was almost a foregone conclusion, when the jury retired at 7.20 pm. Just 10 minutes later they were back again with a guilty verdict, which, according to the *Crewe Chronicle*, moved everyone in the courtroom, except Bevan, who displayed the cold callousness that had marked his every public appearance. Within 10 minutes of the judge donning the black cap to sentence him to death, Bevan was on the 7.42 train to Knutsford. It was reported that on arrival the recently condemned prisoner slept from 10.00 pm until woken at 6.30 am next day.

Living in the shadow of his impending execution, fixed for 16 August 1887, did have an effect upon Bevan. He made a full and free confession to the Revd W Truss, the prison chaplain, of his guilt, both in the death of his aunt for the money in her purse, as well as his intention to kill Mary Jones. This confession also enabled the chaplain, and the deputy governor of the prison, to visit Coppenhall to locate the missing purse containing the pitifully small amount of just over 16s. Much of the rest of the time Bevan spent in writing letters and copying hymns and prayers. Apparently, the imminence of death had wrought a degree of penitence that had never been part of his persona previously. He requested visits from his relatives, in order to express his sorrow, though not all found the grace or compassion to answer the call.

Meanwhile, life continued as normal in the town of Crewe, as the LNWR and the council organised events to mark the jubilee of the town, which included the LNWR's gift of the Queen's Park. An attempted murder in Audlem was the current news, along with the death of Bartholomew Kean, the company's chief storekeeper. There was a letter in the *Chronicle* from lamp-lighter Clark, but that was not unusual. Very little notice was taken of an eccentric man who used Crewe as a staging point in his journey, wheeling a barrow across the United Kingdom.

Unnoticed by the world at large, Bevan received visits from a maiden aunt and Thomas and Ellen Clutton.

On the night before his appointment with James Berry, the public executioner, who would receive about £10 for performing the gruesome task, Bevan retired to bed 40 minutes before midnight, after writing eight letters to be posted after his demise. Awakened at 5.30 am, following a restful night, he made his bed and ate a light breakfast, prior to spending time with the Revd Truss. After expressing the hope that his Uncle Henry Griffiths would forgive him, he took his leave of the warders, thanking them for their kindness, as Berry pinioned him preparatory to the walk across the yard to the execution shed. Looking pale and haggard and 4lb lighter than when he was sentenced, Bevan stood on the trap and shook hands with the prison governor while Berry placed the white hood over his head. Before the clock finished striking the hour of 8, the 20-year-old Thomas Henry Bevan had dropped the few feet that suddenly ended his life for the brutal slaying of his Aunt Sarah.

Of the four sisters who had been born in Worthenbury, Flintshire, only Ellen stayed on in Crewe. By 1901, James and Elizabeth Parsons had moved away, though three of their five children were lodging in the Henry Street house, which was now tenanted by Thomas Hulme married to Mary (formerly Parsons). Ellen and Thomas Clutton had moved out of Orchard Place into a nearby house in West Street, and were living there with their widowed daughter Ellen and her daughter Eleanor. Henry Griffiths cannot be found on the 1891 census. By then he would have been 67, which, though not old by today's standards, was an age that many men of that era did not reach. If he was dead, he certainly did not pass out of this world in the terrible and evil way that his unfortunate wife Sarah did while living in Henry Street.

Chapter 11

Who Killed His Father With An Axe?

Without a doubt, the murder that excited the local and national press more than any other that has occurred in Crewe was the killing of Richard Davies by his two sons, Richard and George, in January 1890. The only crimes to reach the columns of the *Crewe Chronicle* in the first weeks of that year were the usual crop of public-order misdemeanours, which included John Nield, a regular offender, who had been teetotal since Christmas and promised to sign the pledge, as drink always brought trouble. So it was that the violent death of a prominent Crewe tradesman created a sensation that ripped through the town like a winter gale.

Richard Davies, who was born in 1839, trained as a tailor, rising to foreman with the Crewe Co-operative Society. Sometime in the late 1860s, he set up on his own account as a tailor and draper at premises at the east end of Victoria Street. Owing to his business acumen, the venture thrived to such an extent that he was able to purchase four other shop premises, in Heath Street and Market Street. In about 1879, a further speculation saw him purchase a 5-acre farm at the Hough, which was used as the family home. Meanwhile, he opened another shop at 85 Victoria Street, which became his main business, as well as his residence for most of the week.

Marrying his wife, Mary, in September 1862, his family eventually numbered six boys and two girls, all of whom were expected to work for little reward in the family business. John,

Three members of the Davies family. (Cheshire Archives and Local Studies)

the eldest son, earned his father's severe displeasure when he obtained a job with a rival, namely Charles Vickers, of High Street and Victoria Street. His eldest daughter also tired of being her father's drudge and married Thomas Palin in 1886, so upsetting him that he never spoke to her again. In 1885, an apprentice with Richard Davies was so disgruntled with the treatment he received from the tailor that he reneged on his indentures, only to be sued by Davies for breaching the agreement.

The basic details of the murder are simple in the extreme. He was killed by several blows to the head while returning to the family home at the Hough, after leaving Victoria Street at 9.30 pm on Saturday, 25 January 1890. Accompanying him in the small trap, or dog-cart, was George Davies, his 16-year-old son, who raised the alarm at about 11.15 pm. George ran into the farmhouse, which fronted what is now the A52, forever disturbing the family with the cry that his father had been stopped by two men.

Richard, an older brother who had arrived home about 10 minutes before, dashed out to Crewe Lane, where the crime had been committed, only to return with the pony and trap to inform his mother he was going for the police. She waited in the home of her eldest son, John, until Richard returned with the police and the corpse of Richard Davies senior. John Davies had found the body of his father on the right-hand side of Crewe Lane, against the hedge bank. Bathed in the light of borrowed lanterns, the immediate scene was covered in blood from the severe cuts that had almost severed the head from the body.

On John's instructions, Richard drove the trap to the police station, in Edleston Road, before calling at the shop in Victoria Street to break the news to his sister, Emily. Afterwards he returned to the Hough, in company with the police, to view the murder scene, where a small party of men, with John Davies and his brother George, were keeping watch. Knowing that little could be achieved in the darkness, Inspector Oldham allowed the Davies brothers to carry the body back to the family home, where it remained until removed for a post-mortem examination.

Meanwhile, responsibility for the police investigation was moved up the ladder of command, until reaching Colonel Hammersley, the Chief Constable of Cheshire, as such a diabolical event was creating massive interest across the country. Initially, the story of two attackers was half believed, especially when it emerged that Davies had been attacked at the same spot a few years before. At that time, the combined efforts of Richard senior and his eldest son John, armed with a milking stool, drove the assailants away. Inspector Oldham instituted a search of all lodging houses within a 40-mile radius, arresting a couple of tramps in the process and holding them until they could prove their innocence.

When, under cross-examination, the brothers' stories showed several inconsistencies the police increased the pressure on the two teenagers, in addition to searching the Victoria Street premises and questioning Emily Davies, who resided there. Aware that an axe, used for chopping wood, was missing from the rear of the shop, Superintendent Leah interrogated the brothers, under caution. On Thursday, 30 January, after over a day of solitary confinement and intensive questioning, the brothers eventually confessed to the slaying, with each blaming the other. What seems to have started off as mild speculation regarding killing their father had quickly developed into a definite plan.

It was on this day, the penultimate day of January, that Richard Davies was buried in the small graveyard of the Congregational church at Haslington, which was built in the early years of the nineteenth century. This village was the boyhood home of Davies. Graves were not frequently needed in this denominational burial ground, a fact that was emphasised when it was found that the grave had been dug too small for the coffin. The Revd A W Potts, minister of the Hightown Congregational church, had to retreat back to the church, along with the mourning party, while extra space was created in the grave.

After several appearances at the local magistrates' court, the prisoners were committed to the Spring Assizes, at Chester, where they were tried before Mr Justice Wills. All the evidence presented showed both brothers were equally involved. It is possible that the previous attempt to stop and rob the trap by persons unknown fixed the location for the murder. Richard maintained his usual routine of leaving the shop earlier than his father, but instead of going home went to the skating rink, in Earle Street. Knowing his father's habits, he left in time to hide in Crewe Lane, until the arrival of the trap carrying his father and brother George. Here the stories differ, as both denied striking the death-dealing blows. On the balance of the evidence, it would appear that George swung the axe after Richard stopped the pony, by the side of the road. Once the deed was done, Richard went home, as normal, to await the return of George with the dreadful news.

At the preliminary hearings, Mrs Davies had suggested that the family lived happily at the Hough, with good relations all round. The *Crewe Chronicle* even suggested that Richard Davies was a good, kind man, respected by everybody. A much different picture emerged at the trial, instigated, in part, by a letter in which Richard pleaded with his mother to tell the truth about the treatment she received at the hands of her violent husband. Pertinently, Richard also wrote that they had determined to kill their father because of his bad behaviour towards them all.

Apparently, Richard Davies senior was a tyrant who only allowed his daughter, Emily, 13s a week to cover housekeeping expenses, yet demanded that his meals should include meat every day. He always ate apart from the family. Under cross-examination, Mrs Davies admitted she had no access to money, meaning that she and the children often went hungry, despite having to work at the tasks he set them. Sending the younger children to Sunday school often called down his wrath, leading to verbal and physical abuse, with Davies sometimes pointing a gun and threatening to shoot his wife. Of a very moody disposition, she never knew how he would react on any occasion,

The murder scene in Crewe Lane. (Cheshire Archives and Local Studies)

being particularly brutal when he had lost money at the races, where it seems he fancied himself as a bookmaker.

This account of the family's experience of Richard Davies, unseen by the outside world, caused a sensation, especially when compared with the complacent words uttered at the inquest, where his wife had claimed that they were a happy family with nothing to divide them. A couple of sentences from those reported in *The Times*, of 21 March 1890, places Richard's attitude in a sympathetic context: 'Some weeks before my husband died he used serious violence towards me. Richard came down out of his bed, and stood between us, to save me from my husband's violence. Richard was a good son to me.' Such evidence, though not excusing the dreadful event, helps to explain why it occurred.

Over the days following the murder, further evidence emerged that would have brought a guilty verdict without the confessions. First, the handle of the missing family axe, used regularly at Victoria Street, was found buried in an adjacent field, followed, a few days later, by the blade. Close examination revealed that blood had stained the clothes of the two brothers, which is not surprising considering the many wounds to the head and hands of Richard Davies. Dr Frank Matthews, of Nantwich, informed Henry Churton, the coroner, that Davies had six fractures to his skull and ten head wounds, along with severe cuts to his hands, causing blood to flow freely onto the surface of Crewe Lane.

The barrister acting for the older brother worked for a verdict of manslaughter, a line of argument that was received less than sympathetically by the judge in his summing up. After spending less than an hour deliberating, the jury returned to pronounce both brothers guilty of the murder of Richard Davies, with strong recommendations for mercy on account of their youth. Within a few minutes, the boys had received the dreadful sentence that meant their days on earth were numbered, and that they needed to prepare themselves for imminent death.

As executions no longer took place at Chester Prison, the

brothers were taken to Knutsford, which was now the lawful place for Cheshire murderers to be hanged, to await their fate. Even in prison, under sentence of death, the demeanour of George Davies hardly changed. Contemporary reports state that he was stolid, indifferent and unrepentant, to the point where the *Chronicle* reported a strange rumour circulating in the town, that he had asked for a concertina to while away the time. Richard, however, was penitent and troubled. When in prison before the guilty verdict, he wrote to a friend about his feelings: 'I was tempted and overpowered to do wrong. . . . I have confessed truly the part I took in it. May the Lord help it to be proved truly at the trial, and may I meet my punishment bravely.' The letter makes it patently clear that he accepted his part in the murder, though never for one moment did he confess that he had used the axe upon his father.

While the brothers were in the condemned cells at Knutsford, C H Pedley, solicitor to the Davies family, was making great efforts to secure a commutation of the sentence. A frenzied outburst of action resulted in petitions, both locally and nationally. A resident of Highgate, J T Hartshorn, sent a plea for clemency containing 25,000 names, gathered in a matter of days, while another was sent from south Cheshire. Altogether the reprieve agitation yielded 2,000 telegrams, 1,000 letters and petitions containing 150,000 signatures. The recipient, Henry Matthews, Home Secretary in Lord Salisbury's Tory cabinet, reduced George's sentence to penal servitude for life, but remained unmoved regarding the fate of Richard. The difference in ages between the two was only a couple of years, yet, as Richard reached 19 while awaiting trial, Matthews would not consider changing the sentence for him.

Strenuous efforts were made right up to the last day of Richard's life to secure a reprieve for him – his mother even wrote a letter to the Queen – yet all to no avail. After the news of his respite, George was asked by his elder brother John to tell the truth about the slaying and admit that he had used the axe, but George continued to declare his innocence. On hearing that George's sentence had been commuted, Mr A T Jackson, a member of the jury that had found the brothers guilty, wrote to a news agency stating:

> . . . *but by what course of reasoning the Home Secretary has arrived at such an unjust decision I am at a loss to understand. The recommendation of the jury was on behalf of both, and upon the ground of youth only. This, in answer to the Judge, was stated in the most emphatic manner by the foreman of the jury, consequently this can be the only ground for arriving at the decision. Therefore, I should very much like to know why both boys are not treated alike.*

He went on to say that the jury were firmly of the opinion that if one was guiltier than the other, it was George.

The efforts of Pedley and others all came to nothing, and Richard woke at 5.00 am on Tuesday, 8 April 1890 knowing that he would never see another sun rise. Getting up an hour later, he prepared himself for death, with his last confession: 'I truthfully declare in my last hour that I never struck my father on the night of his death and that I never had the axe in my hand.' Six members of the press, who were allowed to witness the proceedings, included a journalist for *The Times*, who had reported the trial. He was now scarcely able to recognise the youth who walked from the condemned cell, so vast were the changes. When he came to pinion the prisoner, Berry, the public executioner, had to bulk up Richard Davies with a blanket, in order to tighten the pinion belt.

An observer reported that the distress on the lad's face could not easily be forgotten. An extra ordeal was the 50yd walk from his cell to the scaffold hut, torment that was relieved only slightly by Berry placing the white hood over his head before he reached the door, thereby preventing Richard from viewing the instrument of his death. His last words were: 'My Lord God I commend my soul to thee. Receive my spirit', words that displayed an attitude condemned by Henry Clark, the eccentric lamp-lighter of Crewe town, when he complained in a letter to the local paper that Christianity offered forgiveness too easily.

The actual execution was soon completed, for by 3 minutes past 8 the black flag was flying on the prison's flagpole, telling the crowd on that cold, wet morning that Richard Davies had paid the ultimate penalty. No doubt his brother George, waking up in that same prison, heard the dreadful tolling of the bell, reciting the same tale as the flag. After an hour, Richard's body was taken down to be viewed by the six journalists, who later described what they had seen for their Victorian readers with such phrases as, 'his hands and face livid', 'marks of the noose encircling his neck' and, most macabre of all, 'his ears turning black'.

His death did not bring instant closure to the case, as questions were asked in the House of Commons in the days immediately following the execution regarding the remission of George and the death of Richard. Walter McLaren, nephew of John Bright, and MP for the Crewe division, considered the Home Secretary's action to be unwise, wrong and cruel. The *Chronicle* commentator was even more trenchant: 'Home Secretary Matthews is himself guilty of legal murder . . . George was the boy who killed his father. That is generally acknowledged.'

In the Commons, Matthews was quick to respond to this Parliamentary storm, declaring that he had included the advice of the trial judge in his decision to respite one and not the other. He was staunchly supported by A J Balfour, a member of the Cabinet, and soon to become prime minister.

In the weeks following, George Davies was removed from Knutsford to Stafford, only to be moved again in February 1891 to Chatham. In March 1905, he breathed the air of freedom when he walked out of Parkhust Prison, after serving fifteen years of his twenty-year stretch, though he did not return to the

The long-demolished Davies farmhouse. (Cheshire Archives and Local Studies)

bosom of his family. According to the book *Criminal Lives*, he migrated to Australia to start a fresh life. Aged 32, he was still a comparatively young man, planning a new start in a new country. What became of him there nobody yet knows.

Meanwhile, Mrs Mary Davies continued to live in the family's farmhouse at the Hough, purchased by Richard Davies many years before. In the summer of 1890 Thomas Cliffe, of Crewe Gates Farm, gave Mary a milking cow to enable her to continue farming in a small way. The stock and fittings from her murdered husband's premises in Victoria Street were auctioned by Gibson, a local auctioneer, six weeks after the funeral. Even the safe was sold, though the keys were still in the hands of the police. A family named Atherton turned 85 Victoria Street into a stationery and fancy goods shop. Davies's four shops at the Heath Street junction with Market Street were purchased by the council in May 1892, at a cost of £1,600, for road-widening purposes. Mary Davies died in September 1897, leaving her three-storey house, with its six bedrooms and 4 acres, to be auctioned by Henry Manley, the Methodist local preacher and auctioneer, of Aston, later that month. The only tangible, local reminder of this dreadful event is the appellation of 'Murder Lane' to the country road where it all happened on that wet and windy night in January 1890.

Chapter 12

From Coppenhall Rectory to Canadian Gallows

While Richard and George Davies were awaiting trial in February 1890 for the murder of their father, another man, John Reginald Birchall, known in the town of Crewe, shot two bullets into the brain of Frederick Benwell, at Eastwood, in Canada. This crime has been included here because of the interest it created locally and nationally.

Reginald Birchall was, in reality, a Walter Mitty character or perhaps, more truthfully, could be described as a conman. Born in 1866 in Oswaldthistle, Lancashire, where his father was the rector of Church Kirk, he was the youngest of five children, there being twenty-four years between him and his eldest brother. He was educated at Rossall School, near Fleetwood, and then at Oxford, where he was asked to leave owing to his unruly lifestyle, funded on the strength of a legacy that he would inherit when he reached the age of 25.

Attractive and charming, especially to ladies, it was rumoured that he was very rich, with an extensive estate in the west of England. According to the same rumours, he had a military background, having served in one of the more fashionable regiments, and wished to be addressed as Captain. Though none of this was true, it did not stop the 'Captain' being received with deference when he condescended to attend the more respectable pubs and cultural events in midland towns, such as Hanley, where he was well known and mixed with effortless grace amongst the great and the good.

In the spring of 1888, Annie Reid and her younger sister Sarah, or Sally as she was known, daughters of the recently deceased the Revd Moses Reid, rector of Coppenhall, went to visit some friends in Cemetery Road, Shelton. This was a suburb of Hanley, one of the north Staffordshire conglomerations of pottery towns. The host and head of the house was James West-Jones, a solicitor and coroner for Hanley. While they were there, the immaculately dressed Birchall, who moved easily from one district to another, came as a guest to the solicitor's table, where he quickly impressed Sally Reid, the protected and gullible daughter of Coppenhall Rectory. Within a few days, the infatuated girl agreed to Birchall's proposal of marriage, seemingly against the advice of her brother, the Revd Cawley Reid, the newly installed rector, as she never returned to the Rectory alive, preferring to stay with the West-Jones until the nuptial day arrived.

Unfortunately, that day never did arrive, for the day of the wedding (postponed twice at the groom's request), finally fixed for 15 April 1888, about a month after they had first met, was the day of her death. Early in April, Sally went on an outing with Mrs West-Jones and her sister, only to get caught in a heavy shower of rain. From this, she developed a cold that quickly turned to pneumonia making her critically ill. Despite many letters and telegrams, Birchall could not be contacted in time to see his would-be bride before she succumbed to the killer illness. Annie Reid even travelled to Oxford, where Birchall was supposed to have rooms in Lincoln College, yet was unable to find him, despite a fervent and frantic search.

On the day of Sally's death, a letter arrived, 'To the fiancée of Reginald Birchall', written in affectionate language and referring in glowing terms to the coming marriage. A letter was all that did appear that month, for he was in absentia, even for the funeral of his bride-to-be, which took place at St Michael's Church,

The Reid family tomb in Coppenhall churchyard. (Peter Ollerhead)

Coppenhall. Her body, dressed in her white wedding gown with orange blossom at her brow, was brought back to lie in the church all night, before being interred with all the rites that a high Anglican funeral service could muster. Much ink had been used in letters to the *Crewe Chronicle* and to the Bishop of Chester, complaining of the Anglo-Catholicism of Father Cawley Reid, the extremely young rector of Coppenhall parish and brother to Sally. How strange that her fiancé, Reginald Birchall, was not amongst the mourners that day, though he did appear a few days later with a wreath to lay at the freshly filled grave on the west side of the churchyard.

A few weeks later, Birchall again visited the West-Jones' home, where he met Florence Stevenson. She was the sister of Mrs Marion West-Jones and daughter to David Stevenson, traffic manager for the LNWR, who was living with his son-in-law at Belsize Park Gardens, London. Florence, a 26-year-old maiden lady, did not long retain the state of spinsterhood, for within a few days she was swept away by the charm and charisma of Reginald Birchall. They eloped and were married before the end of September 1888, six months after the proposed wedding to Sarah Reid.

Whether the wedding failed to bestow the riches that Birchall envisaged or, whether he was simply unable to stop himself acting as a conman, it is certain that, before the end of the year, he embarked upon a get-rich-quick scheme by fleecing immigrants to the crown colony of Canada. With the help of an unsuspecting solicitor, he advertised in newspapers, and other appropriate journals, for a partner in a farming venture in Ontario.

The gist of the scheme was that an unsuspecting Englishman would sign over a sum of money to enter into a partnership in a farm that did not exist. This plan, like all smoke and mirror tricks, depended to a large extent upon the devious charm of the perpetrators. In this case, Frederick C Benwell, of Cheltenham, in response to an advertisement, eventually met Birchall, who was now masquerading as a peer of the realm under the title Lord Somerset – hence the rumours of a large estate in the west of England.

Frederick Benwell, one of eight children, whose family home was Leckhampton Hall, near to Cheltenham, was on the lookout for an opportunity to make money from the colonial lands of the British Empire. Such motivation could have been in his blood, as his father was born in the East Indies and his mother in the Cape of Good Hope. Completely satisfied that Lord Somerset and the land scheme were genuine, Benwell entered into a partnership with Birchall to farm land near to Woodstock, in

Ontario. Birchall even had the documents ratified by Lieutenant-Colonel Benwell, of the 1st Surrey Militia, the father of his victim.

Early in 1890, Birchall, his wife Florence and Fred Benwell sailed from England to New York on the *Britannic*, accompanied by Douglas Pelly, the son of an English clergyman, who appears to have been another potential victim of Birchall's avarice. They stayed for a few nights at Niagra, where Birchall, having visited the area a few times to become familiar with the terrain, was known and recognised as Lord Somerset. From there they moved to Buffalo, where Pelly stated that he saw Benwell and Birchall practising each other's signature. He also testified that Benwell left, after saying he was going to examine the farm, and that he never saw him alive again.

On 21 February, two brothers, George and Joseph Eldridge, found the body of a man with two bullet holes to the head draped over the stump of a fallen tree in a forest about 4 miles from Eastwood station. Immediately they went for William Crosby, the local JP, who, after viewing the body, arranged for it to be taken back to Blenheim, the township in his jurisdiction. The unidentified corpse was buried in Princeton cemetery six days later, by which time J Wilson Murray, chief detective for the province of Ontario, had been brought into the investigation.

Meanwhile, Birchall organised a search for Benwell who, he said, had gone missing, sending Pelly to New York to look for him. While he was away, Birchall went to Princeton to suggest to the undertaker that the unidentified corpse might be his missing friend, Fred Benwell. John Drake, the sexton of the cemetery, opened the grave to allow Birchall a look at the unnamed corpse, and he immediately identified it as that of his friend. Drake also exhumed the corpse on the 6, 7, 8 and 18 March to let other authorities examine the remains. Fortunately, it was very frosty, so decomposition was not too advanced. J Wilson Murray was obviously interested in Birchall, who, unable to allay his suspicions, was further investigated. As a result of these inquiries, Birchall was arrested by Murray Wilson, while in bed with his wife, and charged with the murder of Benwell.

When Pelly returned from New York, he too was interviewed at length, though, as there was no evidence to link him to the shooting, he was later released without charge. In his evidence, Pelly suggested that Birchall had plans to push him into the maelstrom at the foot of Niagra Falls, but was prevented from so doing by the presence of onlookers. The greatly distressed Mrs Florence Birchall, who also came within the purview of the constables' investigations, was able to satisfy them that she was innocent.

The prosecution claimed that Birchall, or Lord Somerset, had arranged to show Fred Benwell the farm that they were supposed to own. They travelled together to Eastwood station, which was little more than a wayside halt, about 100 miles south west of Toronto. From there they walked for about 90 minutes, through thickly wooded terrain, until reaching a swamp, where Birchall shot the unsuspecting young migrant twice in the head.

Leaving the fallen body, Birchall retraced his steps to board another train at Eastwood station for the journey back to Buffalo, where he feigned concern about Benwell's disappearance, sending Pelly on his fruitless trip to New York. As recounted above, after a few days had passed Birchall, pressed by Pelly, who had seen pictures of Benwell's corpse in the local paper, went and identified the body.

It took the police many weeks of patient investigation to discover all the facts about Birchall's advertisements and contacts with solicitors in his scheme to lure the sons of wealthy families who were looking for opportunities to make their fortunes in the newly opened territories of the English colonies. Once the news of Birchall's arrest reached England, David Stevenson, along with Mrs West-Jones, travelled to Ontario to support his daughter, Mrs Florence Birchall, in her hour of need. Another person who made the long journey from the UK was Charles Benwell, brother of the murdered man, who testified

The courtroom scene during Birchall's trial at Woodstock. (Woodstock Museum, Canada)

that his father had provided the money for the supposed land deal engineered by Birchall.

It was September 1890 before Reginald Birchall's trial for the murder of Fred Benwell commenced at the assizes at Woodstock. From the account in *The Times*, the scene was far different to the august procession of judicial procedure that marked the Davies brothers' trial at Chester, a few months before. So intense was the media interest that telephones, costing 25 cents an hour, had been installed, with temporary feeds draped across the courtroom to a transmitter that interfered with the judge's view of the witnesses. These were to placate the intense interest in the trial from such countries as Germany and Italy. It must have seemed a strange reversal of fortune to Birchall to be tried for his life in the same town hall where, at the end of 1888, he had organised a brilliant dance and social event under the name of Lord Somerset.

Each day crowds besieged the entrances, demanding that because they were 'freemen and taxpayers' a seat or at least standing room was their due, as it appeared that places in the courtroom were allocated by influence or money. On the third day, even the witnesses had to fight their way from the street to the door of the town hall, a distance of about 100ft. When the court adjourned for lunch, some witnesses got caught up in the crowd, and so great was the press of onlookers that even the judge was jostled, to such a degree that his robes got torn.

If the legal arguments are stripped to their basics, the prosecution's case was that the body was found where the murder had occurred, whereas the defence argued that the deed was done elsewhere, and the body carried to the swamp. Witnesses had seen the two travelling together to Eastwood from Hamilton, on the Grand Trunk Railway, while others testified that only Lord Somerset returned on a later train. Items, such as a silver pencil case and pencil found in a Wells Fargo deposit box rented to Birchall, were proved, by Charles Benwell, to belong to his brother. That Birchall was a swindling rogue, guilty of false pretences, was established by a variety of documents, including a letter to Benwell's father, hinting that the time had arrived for him to send the £500 to seal the partnership.

An autopsy established that the bullets were fired into the rear of Benwell's skull from close range. Under the corpse were large patches of blood, suggesting that the place of discovery was the scene of the crime. Intense frost and cold had slowed decomposition of the corpse, in fact it was so iced up it took the police 90 minutes to remove Benwell's jacket in preparation for the autopsy. Other witnesses proved that while Birchall tried to suggest that he had never previously visited the area, the manager of the telegraph office at Buffalo stated that he had rented a postal box for six months in 1889.

Despite the defence seeking to cast doubt that the man travelling on the Eastwood train was Birchall, and the incompetence of some of the Crown's witnesses, it was impossible to break the trail of circumstantial evidence that linked Birchall, or Lord Somerset, to the crime. Accusations were made by the defence that the detective in charge of investigations, J Murray Wilson, fed the witnesses information to use at the trial. Further desperation was evident in the behaviour of Lackstock, the defence barrister, when he hectored a 17-year-old servant girl as she gave evidence, much to the severe displeasure of the judge.

During each day of the trial, Birchall displayed the demeanour of a man with no cares, even to the extent of reading a newspaper in the dock. At other times, he carefully made sketches of the various witnesses, including his friend Pelly. The prison at Woodstock, where he was incarcerated during the trial, also doubled as a poor house and an asylum for the insane. Apparently, in the cell next to Birchall was a man who was prone to shrieking and howling at any hour of the day or night, yet none of this seemed to disturb his composure when he appeared each day for his trial.

On the final day, a large crowd descended on the courthouse at Woodstock, including many who had travelled miles by market wagons and buggies. After listening to long speeches from the prosecution and defence counsels, and a detailed summary of the evidence from the judge, the jury retired at 9.53 pm to consider their verdict. After 90 minutes, they were back again with a guilty verdict, which caused the prisoner's wife to faint when told the news. So it was that John Reginald Birchall was sentenced to be hanged on Friday, 14 November 1890 for the murder of Fred C Benwell.

Friends from England, who had provided money for his defence, did what they could to commute the sentence. Florence Benwell, and her sister Mrs West-Jones, immediately appealed via newspaper adverts, and other means, for the local populace

Dundas Street, Woodstock, 1900. The building on the left with the tower is the courtroom. (Woodstock Museum, Canada)

to support them in organising petitions to respite Birchall, yet all to no avail. It must be said that Birchall displayed great affection for his wife and her welfare all through the trial. The prisoner himself seemed to take the sentence philosophically, though always denying any part in the crime. He left a written note stating: 'If after my death there shall appear . . . any confession that I had a hand in the murder of Mr FC Benwell or any personal knowledge of the said murder . . . it is totally fictitious and in no way was ever written by me.' On the night preceding his execution, he slept little, rising at 4.00 am for a hearty meal of mutton chops, eggs and coffee, followed by a large brandy.

Birchall refused the ministrations of a Roman Catholic priest, never having had any time for religion, and the morbid procession started for the gallows. Radcliffe, the hangman, is reported as saying that he would execute Birchall in a way that would suit everyone. This he signally failed to do, as he did not pull the white hood completely over the condemned man's head. While standing on the trap, in front of 300 of Woodstock's inhabitants, Birchall was heard to ask Radcliffe to shake hands with him, and after doing so the hangman pulled the bolt that let Birchall drop to his death.

The murder of Fred Benwell by Reginald Birchall was turned into an episode in a television series based upon the autobiography of J Murray Wilson, modestly titled *Memoirs of a Great Detective*. A ballad, or folk-song, was also composed around the death at the swamp.

So ends the story of John Reginald Birchall, which, perhaps, would not have finished in ignominy and shame if Sally Reid had not received the soaking that brought on pneumonia. Yet, having learned of his desire for easy riches and a life of leisure, it is easy to conclude that Birchall might have brought ignominy and shame to the clerical family in the rectory at Coppenhall. Perhaps the Reid family should have chosen their friends more carefully, as there was a report in *The Times* of 15 November 1890, that James West-Jones, solicitor and coroner for Hanley, had been arrested the previous day for misappropriating £150, belonging to the local branch of the Starr Bowkett Building Society. That was the very day that Birchall, alias 'the Captain', alias 'Lord Somerset', paid with his life for a murder motivated by avarice.

Chapter 13

Murder at the Old Hall

s recorded in Chapter 1, a violent crime had occurred at Bradeley Hall, Haslington, near Crewe, during the time of Henry IV and while it was still owned by the influential Malbon family. Residing at Bradeley Hall from at least 1230 until about 1720, this family practised law at Nantwich through many reigns. The murder that will be discussed in this chapter is certainly not the 'Colonel Mustard, in the library, with a dagger' type of stately home crime, as it revolves around two young men who were the solitary employees of Thomas Astles, a tenant farmer of Bradeley Hall.

In 1817, the Hall and nearly 200 acres of adjoining farm land was sold at auction to John Ford, of Abbey Field, Sandbach. Those sale particulars described the Hall in detail, claiming it had two parlours, a large entrance hall, two pantries, a salting house, a dairy, two cheese rooms, a large kitchen, five bedrooms and a good cellar. Outside were stabling for five horses, shelter for forty cows, an orchard and a garden. By the end of Victoria's reign, however, it had declined to little more than a large farmhouse, similar to many others in the district. County directories of this period record different tenants with almost every issue, further indicating that it had fallen on hard times, even if it remained a favourite meeting point for the local huntsmen.

In 1907 the Hall was occupied by 45-year-old Thomas Astles, his wife Sarah, 10 years his junior, and their 10-year-old son. The victim was Alfred Henry Birtles, of Wistaston Road, Crewe, who would have been 23 years old on Christmas Day 1907. He had wanted to follow his father's trade of metal working, for the London & North West Railway Company, in Crewe, one of the largest railway workshops in the world. However, owing to his indifferent health and rather weak physique, he was rejected by the LNWR and turned instead to agricultural labouring. In this second choice of employment, he proved to be a willing and effective worker for Astles from the day he started at Bradeley Hall. At the trial, it was stated that Birtles had begun working for Astles in November 1905, yet it must have been before that because Birtles is recorded on the Bradeley Hall census return in 1901. Instead of walking the 3 miles to the farm from his home on the south-west fringes of the town, Birtles lived in, only visiting his family when he had an evening off. From all the evidence given at the trial, he was acknowledged to be quiet, good tempered and reliable.

Thomas William Parratt, the perpetrator of the crime, was a youth of 17 years of age who lived with his father and step-mother in Herbert Street, Sydney, less than a mile from his work. Educated at the Anglican Church School, at Crewe Green, he was able to leave at 13 as he had completed all of his standards, indicative of him being reasonably intelligent, even if his step-mother regarded him as a 'little bit simple'. Incidentally, this school at Crewe Green must be the only one in the Crewe area to number three murderers on its roll of old pupils, as the Davies brothers (see Chapter 10) attended there for a time. After leaving school, Parratt worked for his father as a milkman, a situation that ended in failure owing to his 'take it or leave it' attitude. Most of his customers 'left it', meaning that his father's milk round rapidly declined in profitability.

For most of 1906, Parratt had continual rows with his father over the slipshod way he performed his various tasks on the family farm, often running away in a temper to sulk for hours. On one particular day, after his parent's refused to subsidise his

The scene of the murder of Alfred Birtles. (Colin and Mary McLean)

spending, he let the cows out into the lane, leaving them to wander around the neighbourhood. While his step-mother was trying to round them up, he broke the scullery window to gain entrance into the house. Before she returned, he forced the lid off her cashbox to steal the contents, which he squandered in the nearby town of Crewe.

On returning home, he boasted that it would take two Phillips to catch him, Phillips being the name of the local constable. In the event, it only took one policeman to bring him before H Taylor and F Woolridge, at the local Magistrates' Court, where he was bound over for twelve months for theft and house-breaking. One of his relatives was reported as saying that unless he altered his outlook, he would end up on the gallows. After his peevish and petulant attitude exhausted the patience of a couple of local farmers who employed him for a short while, Parratt commenced working as a stockman for Astles at Bradeley Hall at the end of November 1906.

Thomas Astles first intimation that something was wrong at his farm was when Parratt ran up to him in Earle Street, near to the Euston Coffee Tavern, at about 4.00 pm on Friday, 8 March 1907. From the remarkable, yet garbled, tale furnished by the out-of-breath cowman, he realised that something was so badly wrong that it would need the attention of the police. Before returning home, in the company of a passing constable, he sent Parratt to the police station, in Edleston Road, to repeat his account of the robbery to Superintendent Pearson.

The story told to both Astles and the superintendent was that shortly after the farmer and his wife had gone to Crewe, in the pony and trap, a man appeared asking if his master was at home. On receiving a negative answer from Parratt, he said, 'That's all right. That's all I wanted to know', and left, only to return a few minutes later with two companions, who proceeded to enter into the house by means of a ladder and a broken upstairs window. Accompanied by Harry Birtles, he followed the men into the house, only to be shot at by one of them. Without delay, they

Bradeley Hall, Haslington. (Colin and Mary McLean)

both rapidly made their escape, but Parratt was unable to say where Birtles was or what had happened to him.

Within 5 minutes, the superintendent had mustered eight officers, a couple of them mounted, to scour the area for any signs of the gang. He went with Parratt to Bradeley Hall, where he found the crime scene more or less as Parratt had described, with the ladder still leaning against the house wall under a smashed window. Inside were signs of a robbery, with drawers open, contents strewn around and a cashbox smashed. On the floor of one of the rooms was Astles' shotgun, along with recently discharged cartridges. Near to the door was a scrap of paper, covered with almost illegible writing, which was eventually deciphered to read

Dear sir, the men what have done this crime are as follows, J. Walker, H. Green, D. Lewis, all Staffordshire men. If you want to find us out, you must find us out. We have been watching you go for this last two days and now we have got the chance. Goodbye.
Yours truly
D. Lewis

Superintendent Pearson must have immediately realised that he was dealing with a rare gang of thieves, if they identified themselves so readily, whether Staffordshire men or not.

A cursory search of his home suggested to Astles that nothing of value was missing, despite the open drawers and dishevelled state of the rooms. It was also obvious that Birtles was not inside the Hall, so in the growing darkness of a winter's evening a search was made of the immediate environs, but this yielded nothing, except Birtles' cap lying in the yard. Parratt claimed that he had not seen him after he turned to run away, when the man with the gun shot at them. Pearson sent a constable to Birtles' parents, in Wistaston Road, to check if, frightened by the shots, he had gone there. On receiving a negative answer, he ordered another wider search, while despatching Parratt to the police station, in company with PC Phillips.

Now well past 6.00 pm, on what had become a stormy evening, a search was not easily accomplished. Yet, within 30 minutes, the body of Birtles was found in the brook at the rear of the house, near to a bridge. A superficial examination of the corpse indicated it was riddled with shot, having half the head blown away with the brains protruding. After arranging for the body to be removed to the mortuary at the Isolation

Hospital, in Middlewich Street, Pearson sent to Helmsville, in West Street, for the police surgeon, Dr Hodgson (later Sir William Hodgson), for a more professional examination of the body to be carried out. As Hodgson was not available, his assistant, Dr Brown, established that Birtles had received four cartridges of shot, one removing the back of his head, the others to his side, heart and abdomen, any of which would have caused instant death.

Meanwhile, Parratt was held all night at Edleston Road, where he still clung to his story of the farm being raided by a gang of three men. On the prisoner being strip-searched, Pearson noticed bloodstains on Parratt's left leg, meaning that his explanation of the crime was even less feasible. He was confronted with further incriminating evidence after the police team searched the farm and fields more thoroughly at daylight on Saturday. Finding a shallow hole, about 18in deep and roughly 6ft long, they adjudged that this was a fruitless attempt by someone to dig a grave. A bloodstained wheelbarrow, found in an outhouse, had obviously been used to transport the body of Birtles from the spot where he had been murdered to the brook where it was discovered.

At about lunchtime on Saturday, 9 March, a troubled and distressed Parratt sent for the Superintendent to make a written confession that led to him being charged at 3.30 pm with the murder of Alfred Henry Birtles. In the confession he records that:

> me and Harry [Birtles] had fallen out about two months ago owing to differences about our work as to who was the boss and we haven't spoken since . . . I climbed the ladder . . . obtained a gun from downstairs . . . I shouted to Harry that it was time to water the cows but he made no reply . . . when he came I fired the gun but not at him . . . he swore at me and came towards me . . . I shot at him . . . only to frighten him . . . When I tipped him into the brook I said, Goodbye Harry. It is your own fault this is done.

A confession, when read in its entirety, that is obviously part fiction and part fact. The hurriedly convened magistrates, namely Harry Hoptroff and E R Bellyse, remanded Parratt, who, according to contemporary reports, now seemed remarkably unconcerned about his crime.

Sunday dawned bright and clear, allowing hundreds, if not thousands, of ghoulish onlookers to examine the environs of Bradeley Hall. As it was near to a public footpath, it was easy for the locals to stroll past and photograph the bridge where the body was found. The *Crewe Chronicle* stated that some of the more morbid amongst the crowd actually prised pellets from the door of the barn, took water from the brook, twigs from the trees and roots from the shallow grave in the orchard as souvenirs of the killing.

Crewe Green School, which was attended by the Davies brothers and Thomas Parratt. (Peter Ollerhead)

At the inquest, presided over by the coroner H C Yates, the jury viewed the body of Harry Birtles before its burial in the family grave at Coppenhall. When Parratt was brought from Stafford Gaol for the inquest, the *Chronicle* reporter noted that he looked very haggard and restless, and also that he was represented by H K Feltham, a Crewe solicitor, who was later appointed town clerk. So great was the local interest that large crowds attended both the judicial inquiry and Birtles' funeral, at St Michael's Anglican Church at Coppenhall. A few days later, Parratt appeared in public again, this time for another hearing at the Magistrates' Court. Once more his demeanour provoked comments, such as 'crying, distressed, haggard', even fainting during the doctor's descriptions of the wounds sustained by Birtles.

At his trial on 11 July 1907, at the assizes in Chester before Lord Chief Justice Alverstone, Parratt was proved to have shot Birtles in the doorway of the barn while hidden behind a wall about 15yd away. After reloading, he walked across to the recumbent form of his work colleague to discharge the shotgun again. His first inclination was to bury the body in the orchard, hence the shallow grave, only to find that this was impossible, owing to the tangle of tree roots in the subsoil. After lifting Birtles' lifeless form into a wheelbarrow, he trundled it through several gates to the bridge over the brook, where he dropped it into the water. Returning to the farm, he trashed some of the rooms to give the impression of a burglary before writing the note that named the perpetrators as Staffordshire men. After these efforts to exonerate himself, he dashed the 2 miles to Crewe in an attempt to find Thomas Astles.

Parratt's counsel pinned his defence on the fact of diminished responsibility, showing that in 1876 the murderer's grandfather had been committed to an asylum for insanity and delusions of various kinds. He produced witnesses, such as John Walford, a neighbouring farmer, who had tried to reason with the young man, only to receive 'an idiotic grin'. Another described how

Parratt, when employed to gather pears, climbed to the top of the tree shouting, 'I can sing cuckoo now the cuckoo has gone away', and stayed there whistling for 10 minutes, before climbing down and running away.

His father, who at first refused to appear, said that his son had always displayed a wilful and disobedient streak, despite much chastisement. On being asked by the noble judge to enlarge on the nature of this discipline, the father's answer indicated that it was little more than verbal reprimands, much to the judge's disgust. A representative of Henry Manley and Sons, a local firm of auctioneers, spoke of his unpredictable, uncooperative and stupid behaviour when he was employed by them, though he could not explain why Manley's had provided a good reference for Parratt's next employer.

On being closely observed while on remand at Stafford, the prison doctor's judgement was that Parratt was not insane, only weak-minded, with an unstable nervous system. He was liable to lose control at any time, with a propensity to commit any impulsive act without reason. Medical opinion formed, while he was at Knutsford Gaol, came to the opposite conclusion, with the medical officer testifying that Parratt showed no signs of insanity. In his opinion, the prisoner was manipulative and sharper than most youths of his class and station.

In concluding his speech Mr Trevor Lloyd, defence counsel, argued that Parratt, being subject to homicidal mania, was insane at the time of the murder. He pleaded with the jury for this verdict in order for Parratt to receive treatment while he was in prison. To counter this, Ellis Griffiths, for the prosecution, argued that Parratt was driven by resentment because Birtles would not follow his orders when they worked together on the farm, with robbery as a secondary motive. Within half an hour of their retirement to consider the evidence, the jury returned with a guilty verdict, tempered with a strong recommendation for mercy on account of his youth. Parratt, who had displayed a cold demeanour throughout the trial, listened to Lord Alverstone intoning the dreadful words about being hanged by the neck until he was dead with complete indifference. While in handcuffs, on the way to the Chester railway station, one of the crowd remarked that he seemed as gay as a lark.

Fortunately for the callous youth, his solicitor, H K Feltham, did not adopt the same attitude, as he set to work immediately to procure a commutation of the sentence. A letter to the Home Secretary, Herbert Gladstone, was soon posted to London, along with documents outlining the grounds for mitigation. The *Crewe Chronicle* supported his efforts with such comments as: 'he [Parratt] is evidently mentally short, although the doctors could not rightly class him as insane'. These words give the flavour of the many appeals that were made for clemency. Meanwhile, the prisoner in the condemned cell at Knutsford remained indifferent, eating heartily with no signs of penitence.

Feltham's diligent efforts brought a letter from the Home Office, informing him that the King had been advised to respite the capital sentence, with a view to its commutation to penal servitude for life. A fortnight after he was scheduled for execution, Thomas William Parratt was transferred from Knutsford to Parkhurst Prison to learn a trade, while receiving the ministrations of the penal medical service for his homicidal mania. He remained in the custody of the prison service for almost two decades, having the notoriety of being the last local murderer before the mass slaughter began in France that is known to us as the First World War.

Chapter 14

Persecuting the Poachers

In 1851, the national census revealed that a dramatic change had occurred in England – for the first time more people lived in towns than in the rural areas. Crewe was one of the emerging and growing centres of an urbanised population and the situation had implications for the traditional authority of land owners. With such towns being near landed estates, poaching now began to be practised by men from these urban areas. This brought frustration to gamekeepers and a challenge to the laws against poaching, which were themselves a hangover from the medieval forest laws, even if the penalties were not so draconian.

Though poaching might not come into the category of foul deeds, the punishment meted out for poaching was certainly out of balance with the crime. As a result, the Magistrates' Courts had to be gradually reformed to reflect the balance between land and urban areas. In 1890 a sentence of two months' hard labour for a man found guilty of netting a rabbit was considered excessive by most of Victoria's subjects. Decisions made by the landed classes, who occupied the county magistrates' bench, had to be just and reflect a punishment more in line with those awarded for other offences. At the same time, foul crimes, as foul as any outside of actual murder, were the loathsome ways in which some men treated women, especially their wives. In this chapter examples of both poaching and physical assault will be cited to illustrate the thesis that poaching was over penalised, while some assaults were not punished with the severity they merited.

As an introduction, however, the first case falls into neither category, as it concerns a poaching incident in 1857 when a keeper was murdered, yet where, perhaps, the wrong man was executed. This crime occurred at Tilstone about 8 miles from Crewe, where John Bebbington, gamekeeper for Edwin Corbett of Tilstone Lodge, found evidence that poachers were active on land for which he was responsible. Going out during the early hours of 16 April in an effort to trap the poacher, he never returned alive. His wife must have been used to him being away for long periods of time, as his absence was unreported, or unnoticed, until 5.00 am the next morning, when a man taking a short cut to work found his body in the corner of a field. On examination, it was obvious that he had been slain, as there was a massive injury to his stomach where a shotgun had been discharged at close range. A few yards away were fresh feathers from a recently killed partridge.

Within 2 hours, the police were on the scene searching for clues on the frosty soil and grass on which the body lay. Superintendent F MacDermott, of Eddisbury police, who examined the ground around the body, discovered two sets of footprints, one of which matched the boots of the murdered gamekeeper. At various intervals, across three fields, he was able to detect the second set of prints heading back towards Alpraham, though he lost all sight of them about 1/2 mile from the road or track that led to the village.

By 10.00 am, the superintendent was interviewing John Blagg, a poacher cum-shoemaker of Alpraham, and then returned to the murder scene with Blagg's right boot, leaving him in the custody of a constable. On finding that the sole of the boot matched the impressions left on the soil at intervals between Blagg's cottage and the corner of the field where the crime was committed, he returned to charge the shoemaker with Bebbington's murder. So within 3 hours of being called to view the body, the Superintendent was convinced that he had found the culprit.

Further investigations were carried out over the next few weeks and turned up witnesses, such as James Vickers who lodged with Blagg, willing to swear that the prisoner was out of the house in the early hours, not arriving back until around 5.00 am. William Williams, a neighbour, heard two gunshots at around 4.45 am, while in his garden. He also saw Blagg coming down the track from the direction of the shots. Drinking pals of the accused poacher gave testimony that on a few occasions he had threatened to kill Bebbington because he had confiscated his gun and physically abused him, the gamekeeper being over 6ft in height. They also admitted, when cross-examined, that Blagg had only uttered these threats when under the influence of drink.

At the assizes, in August 1857, all this evidence was presented in a skilful manner by the prosecuting counsel before the court, presided over by Mr Justice Crowder. The case for the defence revolved around four key factors, the first being that Blagg was

Alpraham, 1905. (Peter Ollerhead)

disliked by the landowning fraternity in general, and Corbett in particular, so that, in the absence of another suspect, Blagg was arrested and charged. Not all landowners fell into this category, as Lord Tollemache allowed Blagg's widow to remain in the cottage at Alpraham until she died some forty years later. Secondly, no cartridges of the type that had killed Bebbington were in Blagg's possession, although a counter argument to this was that the prisoner had once used that type. Thirdly, only the sole of the one boot, taken from Blagg, matched the print on the soil. Lastly, the threats against Bebbington could not be taken seriously, as they were said with bravado after several pints of beer. Questions posed by Brandt, the defending counsel, relating to the dead partridge, along with the evidence of two shots from a gun, were left unanswered by the prosecution.

A few minutes before 7.00 pm the jury retired to consider the evidence. Less than 30 minutes later they returned to pronounce John Blagg guilty of the murder of John Bebbington, causing the judge to sentence him to die by hanging. In the following two weeks, petitions for the sentence to be commuted were raised in Nantwich, Crewe and Tarporley, though all to no avail. A few days before he died, his wife pleaded with him to confess, if he was indeed guilty, only to be answered with a denial, and a statement that he was as innocent of the crime as their baby daughter. He also disclosed, to other visitors, that one of the witnesses 'told damned lies'. It all made little difference to Blagg, who walked to the gallows on that August morning with a firm step. The only time he showed any anxiety was when Calcroft, the executioner, had to kick the bolt three times before he could release the trap, leaving Blagg standing waiting as he did so.

The case was hurled back into the public domain thirty-three years later when a startling letter was received by the *Chester Chronicle* from a Mr Sawers, a merchant with premises in New Orleans and a home in Neston, on the Wirral. He wrote that the rector of New Orleans had heard a confession to the Bebbington murder from a man who had been present at the trial, but had not given evidence. Newspapers, local and national, soon got hold of the story, although it ran out of steam as far as in-depth enquiries were concerned. Churton, the coroner involved in the original inquest, was reported in the *Crewe Chronicle* as being inclined to the view that Blagg was innocent. His reasons were that the shot lodged in the body of Bebbington were of a different size to those used in Blagg's gun. Also, there was a discrepancy in the footprints and Blagg's boot. Other statements were reported that further confused the picture leaving the impression that there was a reasonable doubt that the verdict was safe.

Blagg's widow was convinced that the man who confessed was indeed guilty of the murder, even saying that her husband had known who had committed the crime, yet would not divulge his name. He had further claimed that if he told all he knew his sentence of death would be commuted to transportation, a fate that, as far as he was concerned, was worse than hanging, which would, hopefully, be a swift end. It was a matter of sorrow for widow Blagg that the whole wretched saga was back on the front pages, as her only desire was for things to return to normal. In spite of her wishes, the newspapers on the abolition side of the hanging debate made the most of the controversy in their subsequent issues, until they too moved on to new topics. If we shall never know who actually committed the murder, it is clear that one of the factors that placed Blagg on the scaffold was the prejudice against poachers from the landowners of Cheshire.

This prejudice is also evident in less serious cases that were committed nearer to the town of Crewe. In August 1890 Baron von Schroder and T L Boote were administering justice at the local Magistrates' Court to George Beech, Thomas Woodcote and Charles Dooley, who had been seen on land at Hankelow. The local gamekeeper reckoned there were hares, partridges, pheasants and rabbits in the field where these men were found carrying nets, pegs and a long bludgeon. As they were only about 6yd from the road, their defence was that they were sheltering in a barn. As none of them had any birds or rabbits, and Woodcote denied being there, it was only Dooley's confession that he was after a few rabbits that introduced a positive note into the case. After due consideration, the county magistrates gave Beech and Woodcote one month's hard labour each and Dooley six weeks. The editor of the *Crewe Chronicle* commented that: 'Six weeks imprisonment for looking for a rabbit is barbarous . . . Even poachers are entitled to fair play and we think that as game preservers the magistrates ought to have left this case to other justices to deal with.' Baron von Schroder lived at the Rookery, Worleston, amidst his hundreds of acres, while Thomas L Boote's home was Corbrook House, Hatherton, about 2 miles from the field rich in game.

In 1886, four years before this case, von Schroder was again a magistrate, along with Colonel Cotton and L D Broughton, all owners of large estates, when two men were brought before them charged with killing a hare on the land of Wilbraham Tollemache JP. Despite a high probability of innocence, the men, after being found guilty, were sentenced to a fine of £5 each or two months' hard labour. Considering the average wage for a skilled man in Crewe railway works was around 25s a week, the fine would have been equivalent to a month's income. Baron von Schroder told the defence solicitor that he could always appeal if he did not like the verdict or penalty. Unfortunately, as the men were poor, appealing was not an option as they could not afford it.

About two months earlier, Thomas Dickenson and Jesse Cartwright were awarded a fine of £2 each, or one month's hard labour, for trespassing in pursuit of game on the land of John Charlesworth of Leighton. As the magistrates, Captain Massey, T L Boote, Colonel Cotton and J Bayley, were landowners, with a penchant for hunting and shooting, they were not minded to

Crewe Hall, the ancestral home of Lord Crewe. (Peter Ollerhead)

give the luckless trespassers time to pay. When Charlesworth himself appeared in the dock, before a different bench of magistrates, he was treated far more leniently with a 5s fine for driving his horse and trap furiously along West Street while intoxicated.

The largest estate, nearest to the town, comprised hundreds of acres owned by Lord Crewe. Unfortunately, for the local poachers this also had the keenest of keepers, namely the eagle-eyed John Thomas Slinn. It is not possible to consider all the prosecutions initiated by this man, so only a representative sample will be cited here. Keeper Slinn was involved in two prosecutions on the same day in November 1875. The first was against an old poacher, John Jervis, who was charged with using dogs for the purpose of taking game. Slinn, who gave chase after espying him trying to catch a hare, would not have caught him except for the intervention of an underkeeper. The penalty was £3 plus costs, about four week's wages for a railway porter of that era. At the same court, two brothers, William and John Smith, were charged with a similar offence, where Slinn was again chief prosecution witness. This time, the fine was £2 each plus costs or two months' hard labour. Poaching carried the risk of deep financial penalties compared with being drunk and disorderly or even assault.

In 1890, early one November morning, William Clark was caught by Slinn and his underkeepers carrying a rabbit, some nets, a stone, a bludgeon and pegs. He was the only one seized when the keepers gave chase to a gang of four men, and, as usual, the magistrates jacked up the penalty when contrasted with other crimes at the court that day, fining the luckless Clark £5 plus nearly another £1 for costs. Two months' hard labour was offered as an alternative, if he could not pay. Some months later, a lesser sentence of six weeks' hard labour was given to a local man found guilty of sexually assaulting a 6-year-old girl. There seemed to be a discrepancy in values in those far off days.

Slinn appeared at the Magistrates' Court again three years later, when he failed to identify any of the three men who had been arrested for poaching on Lord Crewe's estate. Apparently, Slinn, along with his brother and six others, had been lying in wait as four men were setting up nets near to the Temple of Peace, at the rear of Crewe Hall. When Slinn called for his party to detain the rabbit catchers, another eight men suddenly appeared at the behest of one of the poachers, who then began

An artist's impression of John Thomas Slinn, gamekeeper for Lord Crewe.
Gladden's Cheshire Folk *devotes a chapter to a thinly disguised Slinn.* (Peter
Ollerhead)

to throw stones at the keepers, causing them to retreat to the safety of the stables.

Later that day, three men were detained by the police, only to be released on bail after 24 hours as no magistrate could be persuaded to attend to the matter. Three days later, the three men appeared before James Bayley, the only county magistrate that heeded the call to occupy the bench, at Crewe. When Slinn appeared at court he was unable to identify positively the prisoners as those that were catching rabbits on the Crewe estate, ensuring that the three detainees were released immediately.

The *Crewe Chronicle* aired public concern about unjust treatment of poachers by posing pertinent questions about this case in the edition dated 12 August 1893: 'Why could not the keeper's movements be accelerated? Why could he not identify them on Monday? Is he so important a personage that the three men have to wait three days before he can identify them?' One week before this, the *Chronicle* had ripped into the county administration of justice with the following opinion in the Notes and Comments column: 'a magistrate is a man of property, whether endowed with natural gifts or not; a man of field sports and indisposed as a rule to treat a poacher with anything like misplaced tenderness or indulgence . . . The magistracy consequently and naturally has become a mere landowning caste . . . In Cheshire there are 320 magistrates, 273 of whom are Tories.' Other similar comments could be quoted from the issue of 19 August, but these are sufficient to project the disquiet that was felt towards the courts' treatment of poachers.

In 1890, there was an official inquiry into the conduct of the county constabulary, part of which involved an examination of the force's attitude to poaching. It was proved that in some areas a private fund was organised by landowners (including some magistrates) to reward constables if poachers were prosecuted and convicted. Sometimes, police were taken off their normal beat patrols to assist gamekeepers, as the report makes clear: 'The police have . . . in the last fourteen years, been employed, to the neglect of their proper duties, in aiding gamekeepers at night . . . on private lands, their beats being meanwhile totally unprotected . . . it is part of the police system to conceal the fact of so doing by entries in their journals misleading the Government Inspector of Police'. Needless to say, all such practices were stopped immediately the report was published.

To close this chapter, and to emphasise that some men committed serious crimes against their wives without suffering the consequences to the same degree as poachers, two incidents from 1882 will be given as examples. One concerns a man who thrashed his wife after returning home from the pub simply because she had forgotten to buy his tobacco. Next morning, when he got out of bed, he threw her washing into the yard, before savagely beating her again, in addition to pulling her around the house by her hair. A further two beatings followed before he went out in the evening, returning in the early morning worse for drink with another man in the same condition. He ordered the poor woman to prepare a meal for both of them, which she did, only to be physically abused again, before being turned out of her home. When the case came to court the magistrates decided that a fit punishment for the man was to be bound over with a £10 surety or fourteen days' hard labour.

In the previous month another case of domestic assault had come before the magistrates. A man from Market Street, who had been married for twenty-one years and had a long history of violence towards his partially paralysed wife, was summoned for kicking her with his clogs. On arriving home one evening, he ordered his wife to remove his clogs, so the defenceless lady did so, only for the heartless bully to use them as a weapon against her as she knelt at his feet. Despite much evidence of continual assault and verbal threats that he would gladly hasten her death, the mayor levied a fine of 10*s* against the husband, but would not grant a separation order. No doubt these wives would rather their husbands had been prosecuted for poaching. It took many years of campaigning before women established for themselves protection from violence in the matrimonial home.

Chapter 15

Only Worse Off if Dead!

As this book is one in a series entitled 'Foul Deeds and Suspicious Deaths', we have no hesitation about including a chapter about crimes against children. In the following pages, the loathsome and despicable actions of a few adults towards children will be cited as examples of violation of the helpless and dependent. These are but representative samples of many that could be mentioned.

It was late into Victoria's reign before the first Act was framed to protect specifically children from abuse and neglect, enabling the state to pry into relations between a child and its parents. Known by some as the Children's Charter, it was considered state interference with the traditional liberties of a free-born Englishman by lamp-lighter Clark of Crewe. That the police now had powers to enter a home if they had suspicions that a child was in danger was, according to Clark, a retrograde step.

A Society to Prevent Cruelty to Children, formed some five years before this parliamentary bill, helped to publicise the dreadful conditions that some children had to endure. This organisation, which became the NSPCC, had an inspector in Crewe by 1902, the same year that a local branch of the society was established. This came about following a meeting that was addressed by the founder, the Revd Benjamin Waugh, at Berkley Towers, the home of A S Day, an animal medicine manufacturer. Needless to say, the chairman and committee of the local branch were from the upper echelons of south Cheshire society.

When Henry Turner, a boot-maker of Earle Street and Oak Street, was summoned in July 1891 he was the first Crewe parent to be prosecuted under the Children's Act. A better case could have been chosen, as this one had features that lamp-lighter Clark would have criticised as leading society onto a downward slope. Turner was charged with ill treating his 12-year-old son one Saturday at around 11.30 pm. Neighbours told the court that they heard pitiful screams and crying, lasting about 15 minutes, coming from Turner's house in Oak Street.

When the police examined Henry Turner (junior) at his school, they found severe bruising to his shoulder, hips and stomach, caused by the buckle end of a belt. Henry Turner, in his apology to the court, said that he was ashamed when he saw the severity of what he had done. Apparently, the boy having been left in charge of the shop, decided to help himself to a portion of the takings before going on a jaunt with his friends. When his father found the shop empty and unsupervised, with cash missing, he waited impatiently for the hours to pass until Henry returned, at well past 11.00 pm, which is when the chastisement took place.

What made this a poor choice for the first local use of ground-breaking legislation was an appearance at the Magistrates' Court hardly one week later, when the 12-year-old Henry Turner was in the dock for a felony. He had been caught stealing money from clothes while the owners were in the swimming pool in Mill Street. The LNWR, which owned the baths, wanted an example made of Turner, owing to the prevalence of theft from the changing room. As he had already received three strokes of the birch rod in 1889, he was sent to Stafford Gaol for a week before entering a reformatory for four years. Many parents in Victorian Crewe would have agreed with the summary punishment from his father, not the prosecution fostered by the infant NSPCC.

Amongst other cases of neglect that reached the Magistrates' Court, just two years after Henry Turner, was that of a couple who resided in Whitegates, a festering slum behind the market.

Sandbach Street, one of many erected by the railway company. It was the home of lamp-lighter Clark. (Peter Ollerhead)

John and Martha Kirk were prosecuted for causing unnecessary suffering to their children, Emily (10), Robert (8), Francis (7), William (5) and Henry (2). Horatio Lloyd, of the NSPCC Liverpool branch, visited the Kirk home on 16 June 1893, where he found the family living in the most deplorable and wretched condition. All the children were covered in sores and vermin bites. In the back kitchen was a quantity of liquid giving off a most offensive stench. Upstairs lay a rotten mattress heaving with vermin, upon which the whole family slept.

Martha Kirk blamed the neglect on the fact that her husband had lost his job six months before. She freely admitted they lived on the charity of others, but declared that her children were not undernourished, a claim with which Dr Wilson agreed. As John Kirk had been missing for a week, Martha and the children were admitted to the workhouse at Nantwich until he returned. When he did, he was summoned to appear before the magistrates who, after listening to the facts, sentenced the couple to six weeks' hard labour for their callous disregard of the children in their care.

Sometimes, children suffered neglect because of the drunken habits of the mother. An example of this is Ruth Butterworth, who first came to the notice of the authorities in December 1902, when she and her husband, James, were summoned for the wilful neglect of their children. Inspector Williams, of the NSPCC, had received numerous complaints about the lack of care in the Butterworth's home in Oakley Street. All the children were poorly clad, dreadfully undernourished and the house was filthy, with little in the way of furniture or utensils. Upstairs there was one bed to cater for the parents and four children, a rotten mattress and a few rags as covers, even in the depths of the winter. A foul stench pervaded the whole house.

Jonas Potts, a Crewe builder, gave evidence that Butterworth was a good worker, earning around 30s a week in the summer months, dropping to 20s in the winter. The mayor, who stated that it was one of the worst cases they had ever considered, blamed Ruth Butterworth's drunken habits for the neglect. Her penalty was twenty-one days' hard labour, along with a severe warning to mend her ways.

Perhaps a measure of blame can be levied against her parents, as her father, John Gresty, was summoned in 1880 by Peter Rannicar, the school-attendance officer, for allowing his daughter, Ruth, to miss 130 sessions out of 200. (Anyone with an interest in the minutia of Crewe's history might be interested to learn that Rannicar, who was son-in-law to George Wallis, was drowned while skating on Betley Mere.) Ruth Gresty married James Butterworth in 1890.

In December 1904, an inspection of the Butterworth home, now in Peel Street, culminated in Ruth being called before A G Hill, Henry Taylor and James Robertson to explain herself. Despite the best efforts of her solicitor, H S K Feltham, it was impossible to mount any defence against being found drunk at midnight, on the pavement in Salisbury Avenue, with her baby Mary Jane, about 8 weeks old, alongside her.

When it came to a recital of the condition of the children, there was, again, little defence that could be offered. All of them were filthy, poorly clothed and emaciated. Arthur, aged 6, had an extensive patch of weeping sores on his right shoulder that discharged so profusely his shirt was crusted with matter. Similar scabs covered his right leg. Mary Jane, the baby, had bronchitis, yet no medical aid had been sought.

A torn, stinking, wet mattress, covered with an old ragged coat, acted as a bed for the children. No other furniture was present, either there or in the other room, where Ruth and James slept on a bed no better than the one provided for the children. According to the police testimony, the youngsters could only be worse off if they were dead. One month before this, the police had picked up Ruth Butterworth asleep in Peel Street, with her baby crying and cold alongside her. James Robertson, Crewe's first working man JP, blamed her habitual drunkenness for the neglect of the family, but agreed with the other magistrates for an adjournment, after Feltham had pleaded for the couple to be given another chance.

When James and Ruth Butterworth appeared before the magistrates at the resumed hearing in January 1905, they had moved into a house in Oakley Street, prepared by their neighbours, with furniture provided by John Booth, furniture dealer and medical herbalist, of Hightown. According to the

NSPCC inspector, James Butterworth was trying his best to rectify the slovenly conditions that had marked their previous homes, but Ruth was often dead drunk when he called. She received a serious warning from the magistrates, who, again, adjourned the case to monitor any improvement.

A fortnight later, the bench had to admit that they waited in vain as far as Ruth Butterworth was concerned, for she had pawned all the blankets and pillows that Booth had provided to obtain funds for a drinking spree. When the police called, she was in a drunken stupor, proving once again reformation was unachievable. James Butterworth handed to the constable five pawn tickets for blankets and a dress. On a bitterly cold night, her four children were huddled on a flock mattress, with only a few rags and an old coat to cover them. All of the children received their breakfast from the Mayor's Distress Fund, as she was usually incapable of preparing any.

Elizabeth Butterworth, the eldest daughter, who was living with her grandparents, stated that the pawned dress belonged to her. Her mother swore that she had only done it to obtain money to feed the family, a situation denied by James, as there was sufficient food in the house. He bought everything necessary, as he would not trust her with cash, as it would be wasted on alcohol. Her sentence was two months' hard labour.

In 1906, a similar scene is recorded, when Ruth Butterworth was summoned for sleeping in an outhouse at the rear of a building in Peel Street. To modern minds this might not seem a very serious offence, yet we have to remember that the outhouse was usually the family lavatory. To make a journey down the yard, in the dark of a winter morning, to find a stranger occupying what should have been an empty privy gave some people a tremendous shock, hence the offence. As she had been up before the bench seven days earlier, on a similar charge, her reward was a week in gaol, with a request for her husband to appear along with his wife when she had served her sentence.

James Butterworth refused to heed the magistrates' plea for

him to allow his wife back into the matrimonial home, as she had had many chances to reform. When Ruth Butterworth saw Tom, her 10-year-old son, she wept bitter tears which, even when coupled with the urgings of the court, did not change her husband's mind. According to the police, she was a lazy, drunken woman who never attempted to change her way of life. Inspector Williams, of the NSPCC, stated that, whereas he had helped to reform many inebriates, Ruth Butterworth seemed impossible to rescue. He also remarked that she was incapable of looking after her family, meaning that the home was much happier without her.

This pattern of behaviour continued into the next year, 1907, for in June we find Ruth in court, where she promised to sign the pledge. When she was summoned again for drunkenness four weeks later, she failed to appear. Already familiar with the inside of prison, after receiving two custodial sentences, another fourteen days was her lot. In November, she promised the magistrates that she would never go down West Street again, as when she did it always meant trouble. This time, Fisher Short, the Unitarian minister, put his reputation on the line by pleading for her to be given another chance, as the Temperance Society would offer her all the help she needed. He need not have bothered, as within a short while she was at the bottle again, being found incapable in Clarence Grove. She died in 1908, aged 38, alone, but, hopefully, not completely unmourned by her children.

Occasionally, the conditions in which some children were being reared drew forth an excoriating blast of condemnation, such as that in the *Crewe Chronicle* in 1899:

> *When a police officer went into the house to make enquiries he was glad to escape back into the air. The place was reeking with filth and the heads and bodies of the children were alive with vermin . . . the encrustations of dirt on the bodies of some of*

these poor little ones were half an inch in thickness ... It was a vile place.

This case concerned Henry and Martha Stockton, who were arraigned before the magistrates for unlawfully and wilfully neglecting their eight children.

They lived in a dwelling in Bank Street, rented at 4*s* 6*d* a week. This figure was easily afforded by Stockton, a labourer in the LNWR smithy, where he earned around 30*s* a week. His wife seems to have been mainly responsible for the disgusting conditions that prevailed at Bank Street, as her husband never missed a day's work or any opportunity to undertake overtime.

Inspector Owen, of the NSPCC, visited the house in July, after receiving information from the neighbours. What met his eyes

Mill Street baths, erected by the LNWR in 1866. (Bernard Owen)

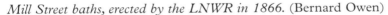

and nose still defies belief, that such conditions could overspread a home in Crewe at the dawn of the twentieth century. Owen said that he had never, in his entire career, witnessed such conditions and neglect, while the policeman who accompanied him was sick and had to light his pipe to mask the stench. Every room was filthy and unsanitary, with poultry having freedom to wander around the house. Upstairs there were two beds in the front room and one in the middle room, all in an abominable state and alive with vermin. Despite the room never having been cleaned for years, it was possible to distinguish blood specks on the walls, where bugs and other vermin had been squashed by the children. All the food that was in the house was half a loaf, a small piece of beef and two eggs.

Each child was examined by Dr John Lawrence, who found that Lizzie (8) was emaciated with a mass of sores upon her head, vermin bites all over and every limb caked with dirt. Her only clothes were a vermin-laden petticoat, a frock, ragged socks and soleless boots. She had been ill for about six weeks and had received no medical attention. Alice (6) had long hair that covered $1/2$in crust of matter, running from a massive sore that was alive with vermin. According to the doctor's report, so numerous were the fleas and nits that her hair seemed to move. Edith (5), Florence (4) and Harry (3) were all in a similar condition. George (13), with vermin crawling all over him, had a large covering of putrefying sores, a diseased ear and a rupture.

At the conclusion of the statements, the magistrates accepted that Henry Stockton bore less blame than his wife, as he was a well-respected employee of the LNWR, having worked at the same job for over twenty-seven years, rarely losing any time. They also accepted that the wife's neglect of the family was not caused by drunkenness, nor were the children starving, as Lizzie's emaciation was caused by illness rather than lack of food. This was about all that H S K Feltham, the defending solicitor, could offer the magistrates in the way of mitigation. Consequently, Henry Stockton was bound over with a surety of

£10, while Martha was sentenced to fourteen days' hard labour.

Despite the attitude of Crewe's lamp-lighter Clark and others, legislation to protect children was a necessary and humanitarian advance for society in Victorian England. Even today, there are regular reports of nasty cases of inhuman action towards young children by those who should be caring for them. Vigilance was as necessary then as it is now.

Chapter 16

Lust, Robbery and Abortion

The case of the missing watch

In the nineteenth century, most of Crewe's crime involved those below the horizon of respectability, meaning that few of the town's more influential inhabitants appeared before the magistrates. To redress the balance, a couple of the cases where persons that were well known locally offended against the moral, or legal, precepts current at the time will be detailed here.

Possibly the most talked about incident locally in the latter years of the nineteenth century was the case of the missing watch, which concerned George Wadsworth, who for many years was an important member of the town's elite. Joining the LNWR in 1852, he was soon promoted to locomotive accountant of the northern section. By 1865, Richard Moon, the LNWR chairman, increased his responsibilities to cover the whole system, not just the northern division, meaning that Wadsworth was in control of a department with hundreds of employees. Chaloner, in his *Social and Economic Development of Crewe*, notes him as one of the most important members of the town's local board, formed in 1860, where his expertise earned him the post of chairman of the finance committee. In 1877, when Crewe was incorporated, Wadsworth was elected on to the first council.

Born in Manchester in 1833, George Wadsworth was 19 when he came to Crewe and 23 when he married a 30-year-old Welsh lady named Ellen Parker. Eventually, they lived in Victoria Street, where Ellen bore him four daughters, Mary, Emily, Susan and Adelaide. In addition to his local board and council activities, Wadsworth was also involved with the Crewe Association for the Prosecution of Felons. He also acted as manager of the LNWR Company's bank in the town. At a lecture in 1876, organised by the Unitarians to criticise the orthodox Christian doctrine of salvation by faith, Wadsworth was amongst those who denounced the lecturer.

By 1883 he was sufficiently affluent to purchase a horse and phaeton to drive himself and his family around the town whenever the need arose. Unfortunately, his skill with the reins did not match his financial acumen for, in October of that year, he was involved in an accident that injured his wife and daughters. Two years later when he retired from the LNWR he

Victoria Street. (Peter Ollerhead)

had to undergo a serious operation, entailing many weeks of recuperation, which prevented his resumption of a normal routine until the beginning of 1886. A year before he retired, while inspecting the council sewage works, he stepped onto a wooden cover over a deep pit of raw sewage that gave way beneath his ample weight. Fortunately, he was saved from dropping into the stinking mixture because his girth was too large to pass through the aperture. From the details of the incident that are outlined below, it could be said that ultimately he fell into a metaphorical sewage pit of his own construction.

According to his account of the incident, George Wadsworth left his home on Tuesday, 11 May 1886 to post some letters before calling at the Mechanics' Institution in Prince Albert Street to read the evening papers and chat in the smoking room. Afterwards, as he strolled along Victoria Street, he was engaged in conversation by a young couple, who remarked that they were pleased to see that he had recovered from his serious illness.

Following this brief conversation, he resumed his walk until he reached Lawrence Street, where the young woman caught up with him and they walked together along Lawrence Street, eventually reaching Gatefield Street. As they stood on the corner, she pushed past him and ran down Delamere Street towards Flag Lane. Thinking no more about it, Wadsworth continued to Flag Lane, down the slope to the crossing with Wistaston Road, where he found that his watch and chain were missing. Next morning he reported the missing items to the police, who displayed 'Reward for a Lost Watch' posters at various points around the town.

Routine police inquiries at Crewe's many pawn shops yielded a result at Richmond and Lees, in Mill Street. A gold Albert and chain, identified by Wadsworth as his, had been pledged for 10*s* by a 'Kate Jones' of Hope Street, who it was discovered did not exist. The sequel occurred at Liverpool, on the 18 May, when Ellis Bradshaw, pawnbroker of Scotland Road, was offered a valuable watch by a pregnant Alice Williams, claiming that it

Lawrence Street, named after a director of the Grand Junction Railway Company. (Peter Ollerhead)

belonged to her father. On estimating its value at around £30, the trader was naturally suspicious and questioned the girl further. She changed her story, saying it belonged to her companion, Kate Fitzpatrick, who was loitering outside, who swore that a man in Crewe had given it to her. After the vigilant pawnbroker contacted the Liverpool police, the disingenuous girls were arrested, pending further inquiries.

Meanwhile, Inspector Downes, of Crewe, had his attention drawn to a paragraph in a Liverpool newspaper about a valuable watch being offered as a pledge. He arranged for Williams and Fitzpatrick to be delivered to the lock-up in Edleston Road. When they appeared before the Crewe magistrates, the 16-year-old Kate Fitzpatrick, who was one of a family of twelve, stoutly maintained that the watch had been given to her as payment for immoral services.

Fitzpatrick's story, so different to Wadsworth's, was heard with delight by the many onlookers at the court, where the councillor was greeted with boos and hisses. She maintained that it was he who engaged her in conversation as she walked along Victoria Street, using certain language and asking her if she felt ticklish. This resulted in the couple walking along Charles Street, across Delamere Street to some vacant land, where they stayed for nearly 30 minutes. Kate testified that he had promised her £2, yet only gave her 2s, which she refused to accept.

Further embarrassing evidence was given by Fitzpatrick, when she stated that Wadsworth wanted to make their clandestine relationship permanent, as he had had such an arrangement with a 'friend' over Liverpool Bridge, who had left the town. Such a situation was impossible, according to Kate, as her father would break every bone in her body if she accepted such an association. She ended by pleading with Wadsworth to tell the truth, so that she could get out of this difficulty, at which point the court erupted into loud applause. The magistrates, while acquitting Williams, committed Fitzpatrick for trial at the Quarter Sessions, with bail set at two sureties of £10. This was immediately supplied by well wishers, along with a solicitor for Fitzpatrick, paid for through a fund opened for public subscription.

Sometime during the following week, Wadsworth arranged an appointment with the solicitor engaged to organise Fitzpatrick's defence, ostensibly to discuss some property business. During the consultation, the conversation moved to the missing watch controversy, when Wadsworth enquired if the matter could be settled out of court. He was informed that the magistrates' decision was final, meaning that he and she would have to have their day at the Quarter Sessions. By this date, Wadsworth had also written to the *Crewe Chronicle*, claiming he was innocent of the scurrilous accusations levied against him by Fitzpatrick.

At the beginning of July, the prisoner surrendered her bail to appear at Chester Castle for trial under the jurisdiction of Judge Wynne Ffoulkes. The case for Fitzpatrick was that Wadsworth gave the watch to her as payment for immoral acts committed near to Delamere Street, whereas the prosecution sought to construct an image of Wadsworth as a man of integrity and dedicated to public service. It was easy to prove the public-service element, for, as we have seen, he was a member of the local board and the town's council. Regarding integrity, the defence named many ladies, suggesting that he knew them in a carnal way rather than socially, all of which was denied by Wadsworth, though no evidence was called to substantiate the denials. It was also hinted that he had resigned from the LNWR following an enquiry into him being found in his office after hours with a lady, allegations that he again denied. Once, it was alleged, he had been assaulted by a Mr Pugh, who discovered him in a compromising position with his (Pugh's) wife.

Further pertinent questions were asked of Wadsworth, such as how did the girl remove his watch and chain from his pocket. Desperate, even ridiculous, was the answer that he must have left it dangling by the chain. Why, if he thought she had stolen it, did he agree to the 'Lost and Reward' notice, issued by the police? His goose was cooked, as far as those in the public gallery were concerned, when Fitzpatrick claimed that he gave her the watch after she had refused the 2s. A few minutes after they had retired, the jury returned with a not-guilty verdict for Kate Fitzpatrick.

This was not the end of the legal profession's involvement in Wadsworth's watch, as they were in court again before the year was out, wrangling over its ownership. Now the number of claimants had risen to three, for Ellis Bradshaw, pawnbroker of Liverpool, declared his interest, with obviously Fitzpatrick and Wadsworth seeking possession. After long and protracted argument, the jury failed to reach a decision.

Crewe Mechanics' Institution, Prince Albert Street. (Bernard Owen)

By the time this case came to court Wadsworth had sold his house in Victoria Street for £950 in order to move to Field Grove in Longsight, Manchester, and take a job as an accountant. He had retired from the council and the *Chronicle* succinctly wrote in October 1886: 'It is scarcely expected that [Mr George Wadsworth] will again go in for municipal honours.' However, after about three years, he returned to Crewe and bought a house called Rose Villa in Hungerford Road, and began working for South Cheshire Brewery as an accountant, which he continued to do until he died in 1892. By 1901, two of his daughters were in service in Stockport, while his wife was living with another daughter and son-in-law in Wellington Square. Ellen, who by this time was suffering from dementia, followed her husband into the family grave in Crewe Cemetery in July 1906, aged 80.

The doctor's dilemma

Amongst the town's medical men in the early years of the twentieth century was Dr John Bond, of Union Street, who had lived in Crewe for over twenty-eight years. Born in Dublin in 1848 and educated for the medical profession in Ireland and Edinburgh, his name was entered into the medical register in 1872. Before moving to Lancashire, where he met his wife, Ruth, he practised medicine in Lanarkshire. By 1881 he was living at Gresty Lodge, near Crewe, along with his wife and 2-year-old son, John. After his wife died in the 1890s when they were living in Nantwich Road he gave up holding a regular surgery, acting instead as a locum tenens when any of the town's doctors needed a stand-in.

His name was brought abruptly to the notice of Crewe's population when he appeared before Mr J W Wilding, a magistrate, councillor and confectioner, charged with using surgical instruments on Ethel Annie Jones in an attempt to procure a miscarriage. She had called at Bond's house in Union Street in September 1905 seeking the whereabouts of a friend, who worked for him in domestic service. As this friend had left Bond's employ some weeks earlier, Jones was offered the job of domestic servant for the sum of 6s a week, an arrangement that, at the very least, seems rather hurried and somewhat irregular to modern minds. Reading between the lines of the different reports of this case, it would seem that Bond was well known for the number of female servants that soon left his employ.

Ethel Annie Jones, who had lived in Ramsbottom Street for most of her life, could never remember her real father, who had emigrated to America. Her mother remarried Samuel Davies, an employee of the LNWR, although, after a couple of years, she left him and her daughter. Consequently, Ethel was looked after for most of her formative years by her step-father, a not altogether unknown event in Victorian England.

Within a matter of days of her moving into Union Street an illicit relationship had been established between the teenaged Ethel Jones and the 58-year-old doctor, which resulted, according to her testimony, in her becoming pregnant. The *Crewe Guardian* records it rather more quaintly with the sentence: 'From what took place the girl became in a certain condition.' It certainly took place quickly as Jones only started working for Bond in September, yet in less than six weeks she was able to announce that she was expecting a baby. It was established at the assizes that Ethel Jones was no stranger to the wicked ways of men, for, as she admitted, her conduct while living in Ramsbottom Street was 'improper'.

After an operation performed by John Bond in his house in Union Street Ethel Jones was left in great pain and weakness. So poorly was she that Bond consulted with a neighbouring doctor regarding nursing help, which was provided by the Surgical Institute in Edleston Road. Nurse Victoria Littlewood was sent to attend the patient. Her observations led her to report the situation to her principal, Miss Green, who, in turn, informed Dr E C Bailey, of Havelock House. He was so concerned after examining Ethel Jones and consulting with Dr Millar, of Edleston Road, that he sent for the police and a magistrate.

Sometime after midnight a deposition was taken from Ethel Jones in the presence of J W Wilding and Charles Speakman, a solicitor with premises in Coppenhall Terrace. This deposition, and the opinions of Drs Bailey and Millar, led Detective Inspector Sheasby to arrest Bond in the early hours of the morning of 24 October 1905 on suspicion of performing an illegal operation. The prisoner denied that he had done such a thing, protesting that the operation was for medical purposes and was not an abortion.

After being remanded four times to Stafford Gaol, the elderly doctor was eventually given bail on his fifth appearance before the magistrates, in recognition of his £500 and two sureties of £250 each, a sum set by the chief constable. The Magistrates' Court, in Edleston Road, was closed to the general public, despite the crowds that waited outside. Wrapped in a large shawl, the pale and drawn Ethel Jones was a pitiful sight who certainly did not hinder the prosecution's case. In addition to the charge concerning Jones, further information had been obtained regarding another similar operation earlier in the year.

This time the patient was Gertrude Taylor, aged 23, formerly of Bridgnorth, who had been in service at Haslington until she had a quarrel with her employer. She chanced to knock on Bond's door in January 1905, seeking lodgings for the night before catching the train back to Bridgnorth. According to her testimony, she was unaware that the doctor lived there and only stayed when he persuaded her to. According to the evidence of Bond's coachman, however, she asked for Bond directly when he answered the door on the second Wednesday in January 1905. She stayed at Union Street for about ten days before deciding to return home. She never made it at that time as the train was delayed, so she backtracked to Union Street where Bond eventually performed an illegal operation.

The sequel to this was a letter sent some weeks later by Taylor in Bridgnorth to Bond, allegedly informing him that his operation had not been successful and that she was still pregnant. She claimed that he answered with an invitation to return to Crewe for further surgery. At the trial, he denied these letters, though Inspector Sheasby produced a notebook that he had found in the Union Street house in which Bond had recorded that he had written to 'Gerty, at Bridgnorth', a comment that supported Taylor's version. She continued to declare that he had promised her £100 and all his furniture if she burned the letters, a promise that was not kept but which caused gales of laughter when it was repeated in court. Regardless of the claims and counter claims, what is beyond dispute is that Gertrude Taylor was delivered of a child on 28 September 1905. Bond denied responsibility for this child, despite an order for its maintenance being made against him. This Crewe doctor certainly attracted a certain class of lady, for Taylor, under cross-examination, admitted that she led an immoral life.

When the full trial transpired at Chester Assizes before Mr Justice Lawrence in March 1906, the charges that were preferred against Dr John Bond were that he administered drugs to Ethel Annie Jones and that he used instruments for an unlawful purpose. The defence's main strategy was to suggest that the operation was not for an abortion, but to cure another, more common ailment, which was not specified in the reports of the trial prepared for the general public. The prosecution produced various local doctors, such as Millar, Bailey and Hodgson, whereas, to deprecate this argument, Francis Williams put Drs Lappage and Turner, of Nantwich, on the stand, along with A J Wallace, surgeon to the Hospital for Women at Liverpool, who all supported Bond's explanation. When the jury retired to consider the verdict, a few minutes before 8 o'clock on the second day of the trial, it only took half an hour before they returned to pronounce that Bond was guilty as charged. Before sentencing him to three years' penal servitude, Mr Justice Lawrence expressed his agreement with the jury's decision.

As a footnote to this last case, it must be said that unwanted pregnancies and back-street abortions brought much sorrow and pain to some women in the England at that time. The alternatives were a shotgun wedding to a man that, perhaps, they hardly knew or a life bearing the social opprobrium of being an unwed mother.

A typical example with a not-so typical ending occurred locally in 1871 when 17-year-old Ann Folen was accused of murdering her newborn son. She had recently arrived in England from Ireland, seeking her lover who had fled from the Emerald Isle when informed of her condition. She traced him as far as Crewe, from where she was admitted into Nantwich Workhouse for the delivery of her child. After leaving with her baby in May, the story becomes confused, until inquiries were made by the police after a lodging house keeper voiced her suspicions. These investigations proved that the child died somewhere between the workhouse and Willaston station.

Initially, Folen claimed that Patrick (her son) had been buried in Nantwich, but later admitted that she had covered the child's body with clay after he had died. When the case reached the assizes, the jury decided that she was guilty of manslaughter rather than murder.

Another particularly sad case was that of a girl from Samuel Street who had managed to secure a post as secretary on the staff of the *Sun* newspaper in London in 1893. Finding herself pregnant after a foolish relationship, she sent a telegram to a woman in Camden Town, whose name had been given to her. The result of this lady's visit was dreadful internal injuries, days of pain and an early death. The first report of this case, in the *Crewe Chronicle*, stated that her death was due to an accident on the busy streets of the metropolis. Obviously, her family did not want the truth to be known as such a stigma was hard to add to the sorrow of losing a young and successful daughter. Such was the power of social convention and contemporary opinion.

Chapter 17

The Slaughter of the Innocents

One of the most infamous cases in Crewe's short history was not a murder despite the title of this chapter, which is a phrase used by the *Crewe Guardian* to describe the incidents that took place. Though no suspicious deaths occurred, it is still worth recounting the details of the Cross Street brothel case to illustrate that Victorian towns had areas that were not all models of rectitude and propriety. It has also been selected for inclusion as it was a strong factor in the agitation to incorporate Crewe.

Cross Street was south of the heart of the town and linked High Street with Oak Street. It was demolished, along with the neighbouring dwellings in Blackberry Street and Bowling Green, in the middle years of the twentieth century to allow for the construction of the car park on the north side of Oak Street. In the 1870s the Cross Street area had lost whatever respectability it once had, being well known as the location of unofficial common lodging houses that the police and the less morally squeamish called brothels. It must be understood that nearby houses in Oak Street and High Street were the homes of respectable artisans and shopkeepers, so there was much agitation for action against this blot upon the respectable reputation of a solid working class town. Without a doubt Cross Street was a foul locality.

At the beginning of May 1875 a reporter, who investigated the many complaints that were being received about Cross Street, found that: 'many prostitutes come to Crewe weekly from such places as Warrington, Manchester, and Liverpool . . . men congregate all night long as soon as the cloak of night shrouds the deeds of darkness and render the night hideous with their coarse ribald jests and blasphemous language'. He further described his visit that for safety's sake was made in company with a policeman:

> *We walked up the dirty neglected street stopping at one stinking house with eight panes broken in the windows. The panels of the doors are all battered . . . there was no furniture in the first room except an old packing box . . . We looked through a broken window at the back where we could see two undressed men asleep on two chairs . . . upstairs there were a man, woman and three children.*

For the sake of brevity only a few cases that reached the courts in 1875 will be cited as examples of the type of raucous and insulting behaviour that the locals had to withstand.

In February 1875, Thomas Lloyd, a breaksman of Bank Street, was drinking with Mary Vickers in the Golden Lion pub in Cross Street. At her suggestion they went to a nearby house, where he got helplessly drunk. Next day, after recovering somewhat, he charged Vickers with theft after discovering that his watch and chain, valued at £6 10s, had disappeared. Robberies such as this were commonplace as the Cross Street houses were in total darkness once the sun had set. On receipt of the complaint, the police discovered that Vickers had tried to pawn the watch and chain in the nearby town of Nantwich. Being unsuccessful, she hid them in a garden in Hope Street, from where the police retrieved them. For her efforts at theft Mary Vickers received two months' hard labour at the Knutsford Spring Assizes.

Vickers figured prominently in the minor crime league of the town. She was born Mary Jane Davies in 1849 and married Charles Vickers in 1871. Between 1871 and 1890, when she died

Lockitt Street. (Bernard Owen)

at the age of 41, she had seven children. As will be seen, she was not a good mother so it is to her husband's credit that their children never found their way into the law courts.

One of the earliest references to Vickers appears in the local paper and concerns an incident in August 1872. A neighbour burst into Vickers' home in Lockitt Street seeking refuge from her husband, whom she claimed was trying to murder her. When PC Clutton sought to arbitrate in this domestic dispute he was pushed by Maxwell, the violent husband, and broke his leg in the process. Maxwell was prosecuted for assaulting a policeman when, despite his defence that the officer had been over affectionate with his wife, he received two months' hard labour.

Over the next two decades Mary Jane, or 'Slasher' as she was known, appeared before the magistrates many times for drunkenness and immoral conduct. In January 1886 she was convicted of sleeping in an outhouse in Mill Street. In March of that year she was sentenced to twenty-one days' hard labour for indecent behaviour in Cross Street, another fourteen days in July for indecent behaviour in Wistaston and a fine of 2s 6d for drunkenness when she was released. In October she received seven days for again sleeping in a closet in Mill Street and a 5s fine for being drunk and disorderly. She made many other appearances before the bench but those cited here give a flavour of the type of woman who frequented Cross Street.

One week before Vickers robbed Thomas Lloyd another prostitute, Alice Bailey, relieved Charles Whelan of 2s 6d and his tobacco box. When the case came to trial, Whelan claimed he had gone to Cross Street with Bailey for a charitable purpose. A day after Bailey was charged, Emma Pilkington, another woman from the same locality, was remanded to the assizes, where she received six months for stealing £1 1s 6d from Joseph Payne when they went to a house in Blackberry Street. Added to these must be many other men who through personal circumstances could not report that they had suffered loss.

In May of 1875, James Dean of Pedley Street, a one-legged man who could only walk with the aid of a crutch, was seen limping hurriedly from Cross Street with blood pouring from a wound on his brow. Apparently, he had met with Mary Mason, another well-known prostitute, for a few drinks before calling her a sow and a pig. He counter claimed that she had turned violent when he asked her for a drink. After hitting her with his crutch she threw a quart jug at him that cut his temple.

At Dean's request, Henry Laing, assistant to John Kay, a chemist with premises in High Street and West Street, treated the gash. However, once the flow of blood was staunched Dean was off again to deal with Mary Mason, only for the bandage to drop off before he reached her. Further violence was prevented by the police, for the fracas had attracted the attention of many passers-by, who gleefully witnessed this free entertainment. Mason and Dean counter charged each other, resulting in the magistrates dismissing the case with comments that they were both bad characters, with Dean being infamous for drunkenness and violence with his crutch.

On 28 June, Inspector Morris, accompanied by PC Roberts, visited Alice Bailey's Cross Street premises at 1.40 am and found Joseph Pidduck, Mary Vickers and Agnes Kennedy on a bed, with another man lying in the corner of the room. In an adjoining room was Alice Bailey with a man, in addition to her three children. Downstairs, in what was laughingly termed a kitchen and where the stench was indescribable, were three more men. When questioned, Alice Bailey justified her activities by claiming that there were houses more immoral than hers. Joseph Hodgkinson maintained that 'Red Poll's' house was far worse than theirs. This evidence enabled the authorities to obtain an eviction order that had the effect of moving Bailey and Hodgkinson to a house in Blackberry Street.

'Red Poll', really Mary Leslie or 'Sadler', to give her other pseudonym, also lived in Blackberry Street and had many convictions for drunkenness and indecency. Hodgkinson, who in the parlance of the time was Bailey's 'bully', had convictions for vagrancy, felony and for being drunk and disorderly. The women from Leslie's house loitered at the corner of Blackberry Street and Cross Street, accosting male passers-by thus driving respectable persons away from the area.

Mary Mason also appears again in this calendar of crime when she was arrested in July along with Ann Davies, another lady with regular lodgings in Cross Street. Davies was so drunk she could not stand, though her 'bully' was vigorously shaking her. Mason had broken three windows badly cutting her arm in the process. When charged with being drunk and disorderly, Mason denied being under the influence as she had only consumed two-penny worth of port and the same amount of claret. Davies, after admitting consuming whisky, asked for her crimes to be overlooked on account of her child. A fine of 2s 6d plus costs was levied against them. Costs usually increased the penalty by 100 per cent.

In July Ellen Whelan was also prosecuted for stealing half a sovereign from George Allmark, a labourer in Crewe railway works. She met him on the corner of Cross Street at about 11.00 pm, when they walked to land near Edleston Road for an immoral purpose. In one pocket he had 7s 6d, while the other contained a half sovereign. Eventually, after giving her 6d for her services, he stooped to pick up his coat and she ran away. It was then he realised that the half sovereign was missing from his pocket.

Ellen was apprehended in a lodging house in James Street (later Naylor Street) at about 4.00 am by a local constable, who

Adverts from Eardley's Crewe Borough Almanack. *Milton was one of the tradesmen that complained about the moral condition of Cross Street in the 1870s. Later in the century he himself was involved in financial irregularities at the Baptist Church.* (Peter Ollerhead)

escorted her to the lock-up in Eaton Street. Mrs Morris, wife of the police inspector, searched her and found half a sovereign in a pocket under her petticoat, along with two six-penny pieces and four pennies. Despite denying that she had stolen the money, Ellen Whelan was remanded to the next assizes where, as an old offender, she received a sentence of seven years' penal servitude. From the details outlined in this case, it would seem that the going rate for a prostitute's services in Crewe was 6*d* a time. A sentence of seven years' penal servitude for such an offence seems a draconian punishment, even when previous transgressions are considered. At the same assizes, a man aged 54 received six months for sexually molesting a 6-year-old girl.

Also in July, a woman named Lily Dale emerged from Cross Street so drunk that she could hardly stand. Wandering up High Street into Market Street, she soon attracted a crowd that got bigger by the minute. For some reason the psychology of the mass caused them to punch and assault the unfortunate lady with such violence that her hair was pulled out and the clothes stripped off her back. Only the arrival of the police prevented further serious injury. Cross Street seemed to stimulate the worst emotions in Crewe's citizens.

As an answer to the many complaints that were being received, Superintendent Saxton took John Caryl, a jeweller, and Henry Milton, a glazier, both of High Street, to give depositions to the Revd J Folliott regarding the moral pollution of the area. (They were made to wait for over an hour while the reverend gentleman finished his meal.) Caryl testified that as the back of his house looked into Alice Bailey's, in Blackberry Street, his family could not help but see numbers of men and women entering the house at all times. Often they were kept awake by the shrieks and quarrels emanating from the property, as well as being compelled to listen to the foul and obscene language. His three daughters had witnessed Alice Bailey fighting with a man, using a knife as well as her fists, as crowds of 'loose' women assembled to watch the proceedings.

Towards the end of July one of the Cross Street ladies, Mary Leslie, charged Joseph Baker with assault. She claimed that when she was removing her clothes before retiring to bed he threw a piece of stone, weighing several pounds, through her window. On interrogation, she agreed that, whereas she had not seen the defendant throw the heavy stone, she was sure it was him as she saw him running away. She was able to make a positive identification as he had lodged in her house for three years, at which point Baker shouted out that she meant co-habiting not lodging. When Mr Tollemache, the magistrate, asked for witnesses Mary Leslie vehemently declaimed that there were no witnesses as the offence took place at a quarter to three in the morning. To add to this farce of a trial, the prosecuting police officer testified that the court could determine what kind of person Leslie was if they studied her nose. Needless to say, the case was dismissed.

On the night of 3 August an inspector and a constable entered Alice Bailey's 'new' premises in Blackberry Street just after midnight, and there they found two unknown woman sitting on the knees of two men. Upstairs were Alice Bailey and Mary Vickers with four men in various stages of undress, while in the corner of the room were Bailey's three children on a bed of rags. Inspector Morris declared, with perhaps a hint of hyperbole, that he had been through some of the lowest places in London, Manchester and Liverpool yet had never come across anywhere as bad as the house in Blackberry Street. Two nights later another raid was executed at 1.30 am and on this occasion they found a Nantwich man with Alice Bailey. Upstairs was Mary Vickers with a man who claimed he was looking for a night's lodgings.

To further illustrate the immoral character of Hodgkinson and Bailey it is worth summarising the evidence of Mary Vickers who, as we have seen, was much less than perfect. Despite this, she manages to provoke a degree of sympathy when she outlines her fall from grace in her testimony at the assize trial. Apparently she had supported her husband and young family by charring and taking in washing until she met up with Bailey in 1873, when she was 27. Bailey, who was about fifteen years her senior, from then on dominated her to such an extent that she was persuaded to join the throng of women in Blackberry Street, leaving her family to be taken into the workhouse. She claimed that this was when she became addicted to drink. From every shilling earned by prostitution Alice Bailey took 3*d* pence, or 25 per cent of her total takings. Bailey's children aged 11, 6 and 3 years were neglected to the point where they had to beg for food.

Further evidence was secured on 13 August when the police found Bailey drunk on the floor with four men, who said they

Bank Street, which was on the east side of Mill Street. (Cheshire Archives and Local Studies)

were there for a bit of a game. On the following night Alice Bailey and Mary Wilson were discovered in a corner of a room with James Hodgkinson and another man, who refused to give his name, while two other men ran away when challenged.

On the 16th Inspector Morris and Constables Wynne and Davidson obtained further proof, which the *Crewe Guardian* would not print out of respect for the values of the time. This, and the testimonies of Caryl and Milton, was enough to gain a warrant for the arrests of Bailey and Joseph Hodgkinson on the charge of keeping common brothels. Later, when they appeared at the assizes before Mr Justice Maysmoor Williams, Alice described herself as a charwoman and Hodgkinson as a labourer. It made no difference for the evidence was overwhelming, earning them both twelve months' hard labour.

When the trial was over, the *Crewe Chronicle* commended the police: 'Superintendent Saxton deserves the thanks of the public for the vigorous steps he has at length taken to oust the disreputable characters in Cross Street, who have for a series of years been a great annoyance to the families and tradesmen of High Street and a disgrace to the town.' The Nantwich magistrates, who occupied the bench at Crewe, let loose a tirade of censure against the members of the local board for their lack of control over the town's affairs. Tollemache, one of Cheshire's landed gentry, was reported as saying: 'He could not understand for one moment how [the local board] could allow such dens of infamy to exist in Crewe. They had . . . a medical officer, an inspector of nuisances and other officials and not withstanding all of this they had allowed these places to exist . . . it was really a perfect scandal.' The *Crewe Chronicle* would not accept such partisan comments without a counter blast:

Crewe has been insulted by persons who have no right to interfere in local affairs when it transpired that they have the ultimate responsibility for the state of affairs that existed. We say, had we our own bench of justices, men selected for their keen business sense, we should have been spared that shameful and unjust reprimand. Why should the bulk of police business from Crewe be transacted at Nantwich?

As stated earlier, the Cross Street episode led to the shopkeepers and businessmen of Crewe agitating to incorporate the town in order to cut further the ties that bound them to the ancient centre of administration. Crewe was now much larger and economically more viable than Nantwich.

All the property in Cross Street and Blackberry Street was put up for auction in January 1876. It was bought by Hawthorne, the grocer of Earle Street, for a total of £720, an amount that averaged £90 a dwelling. The going rate for similar houses in Mill Street, about a 100yd away, was approximately twice as much.

Unfortunately, Vickers did not mend her ways and she continued to appear before the magistrates. In July 1876 she was even charged with the murder of Susan Price, of Nantwich Road, who died from the effects of an epileptic seizure after being wrestled to the ground during a violent quarrel with Vickers. At the following assizes no evidence was forthcoming that Mary Jane's behaviour was the direct cause of the fit and she was released. She continued to stagger along the downward path of drunkenness and prostitution, working the streets on her own account. No blame could now be levied against Bailey as she never appeared again in conjunction with Vickers. In 1901 Charles, her husband, was residing with his daughter and, except for the occasional lapse into drunkenness, lived the life of an ordinary railway labourer. It is a pity that Mary Jane could not have joined him in this domestic sanctuary. We cannot write that Cross Street was ever completely respectable because more than occasional references to indecent behaviour there were recorded in the *Chronicle*.

References and Acknowledgements

Illustrations
Cheshire Archives and Local Studies (These images reproduced with permission of Cheshire Shared Services and the owner/depositer, to whom copyright is reserved.)
Colin and Mary McLean
Bernard Owen
Woodstock Museum, Canada

Sources
Newspapers

Chester Chronicle
Chester Courant
Crewe Chronicle
Crewe Guardian
The Times

Publications
Booth, P W. *The Ride to Justice in Cheshire 1354*, University of Liverpool, 1991
Godfrey, B, Cox, D and Farrall, S. *Criminal Lives*, Oxford University Press, 2007
Lake, J. *The Great Fire of Nantwich*, Shiva Publishing Ltd, 1983
Murray, J W. *Memoirs of a Great Detective*, Heinemann, 1904
Neild, James. *The State of the Prisons in England, Scotland and*

Wales, John Nichols & Son, 1812

Pegler, Revd G. *The Waters of Crewe*, n.p., 1914

Stevenson, D. *Fifty Years of the London & North Western Railway*, Kessinger Publishing, reprint 2009

Walton, Sylvia. *Middlewich House of Correction*, Middlewich Heritage Society Newsletter, March 2009

Yarwood, D. *Cheshire's Execution Files*, Breedon Books, 2007

Records, documents and journals

Cheshire Record Office:

Records of Cheshire Quarter Sessions and Crewe Petty Sessions

Consistory Court records

Account of Crockett inquest

Cholmondely Archives

Transportation records

Cheshire volumes of *Victoria County History*, published by the Institute of Historical Research, London University

Transactions of the Historic Society of Lancashire and Cheshire, Vol. 118, Star Chamber cases

Chetham Society, *Calendar of County Court Rolls of Chester 1259–1297*

Census returns, 1871–1901

Archives of the Church of Latter-Day Saints

The National Archives:

Records of the Court of Star Chamber

Grand Junction Railway Company Board minutes

With thanks to Olly Chambers, the staff of Crewe Reference Library, especially Katherine Bate, and the staff of Cheshire Record Office for all their assistance.

Index